Fighting Mad

MICHAEL CALVERT

Fighting Mad

Pen & Sword
MILITARY

First published in Great Britain in 1964 by
Jarrolds Publishers (London) Ltd

Published in 2004, in this format, by
PEN & SWORD MILITARY
an imprint of
Pen & Sword Books Limited
47 Church Street
Barnsley
South Yorkshire
S70 2AS

Copyright ©
The Estate of the late Michael Calvert, 1964, 2004

ISBN 1 84415 224 3

The right of The Estate of the late Michael Calvert
to be identified as Author of this Work has been
asserted by him in accordance with the
Copyright, Designs and Patents Act 1988.

A CIP catalogue record for this book
is available from the British Library.

Printed and bound in Great Britain by
CPI UK

Pen & Sword Books Ltd incorporates the imprints of
Pen & Sword Aviation, Pen & Sword Maritime, Pen & Sword Military,
Wharncliffe Local History, Pen & Sword Select,
Pen & Sword Military Classics and Leo Cooper.

For a complete list of Pen & Sword titles please contact:
PEN & SWORD BOOKS LIMITED
47 Church Street, Barnsley, South Yorkshire, S70 2AS, England.
E-mail: enquiries@pen-and-sword.co.uk
Website: www.pen-and-sword.co.uk

Contents

Author's Note

This is my personal story, which tells of some of the things that happened to me before and during the war. I have written it down as I saw it and as I remember it, but I realize that others may have different memories of the incidents mentioned. Two minutes after a road accident people who have seen it can give widely differing accounts of what happened; just think how much room for divergency there would be if they were questioned twenty or more years later. Someone once said that truth is a many-sided diamond and we each see a different facet of it. Facts I have been unsure about I have tried to check and I would like to thank Field Marshal Viscount Slim and Lieutenant-Colonel L. E. O. T. Hart for their help. I have also consulted *The War Against Japan*, Vols. 2 and 3 (H.M. Stationery Office), *Orde Wingate*, by Christopher Sykes (Collins), *Defeat into Victory*, by Field Marshal Viscount Slim (Cassell), and Sir Winston Churchill's *The Second World War* (Cassell). Most of the pictures are by courtesy of the Imperial War Museum.

Publisher's Note

The publishers are grateful for the assistance of Philip Chinnery in the preparation of the revised final chapter of this new edition and other editorial advice.

1

First Step to Adventure

When I was twelve I bet a school friend half a crown that I would become a general before he did. Eighteen years later, in 1943, I was promoted brigadier at the age of thirty and won the bet. I felt pleased at the time but, looking back, I know that I did not really deserve to win, for I am more of a rebel than a general at heart.

In the special conditions of wartime, however, the two can sometimes go together, as they most certainly did in the man who was mainly responsible for my promotion, Orde Wingate. No one I have ever met was less like the popular Blimpish image of a general than Wingate, the audacious, moody, highly strung yet ruthless soldier who founded and led the Chindits, the bush-hatted Special Force which operated behind the Japanese lines in the Burma jungle.

Wingate's unconventional ideas shocked the stick-in-the-mud element among the Army's senior officers. Many of them regarded him as an outsider. I remember in India, in 1943, a lieutenant-general who was too dim to see where my sympathies lay saying to me: 'You know, Michael, we Regulars must stick together against people like Wingate.' Wingate, of course, *was* a Regular, but as far as this general was concerned his 'odd' methods and behaviour put him beyond the pale. Fortunately the brilliant and rebellious ideas Wingate produced outshone all efforts to stifle them and were actively encouraged by men of vision at the top, including Winston Churchill and General Wavell.

Persistent attempts have been made to denigrate Wingate since his death and haughty scorn has been poured on the size of his contribution to the so-called 'Grand Design' of victory. But the fact remains that highly mobile units, travelling light and supplied by air, are now widely used in the armies of the West as a whole and are, in fact, the very

9

basis of the modern British Army. These were the methods Wingate pioneered in Burma with the Chindits and I was proud to be able to help in developing this type of warfare.

My own army career had been regarded as distinctly unusual long before I joined forces with Wingate in Burma. I think the reason was that for years, ever since I left school, I had been preparing myself for the war. I claim no great foresight or mystical powers for predicting the future; I just had this feeling that all the experience of fighting and leadership I could acquire would one day be needed. But I was young and at times I probably went about my self-imposed task in a rumbustious sort of way which created a bad impression among my superiors.

I once overheard one of my pre-war commanding officers grumbling to the adjutant about me.

'Young Calvert always seems to be looking for trouble,' he said. 'I suppose it's the Irish blood in him.' He may well have been right, for my mother was Irish.

My father was a District Commissioner in India and I was born at a place called Rohtak, about forty miles from Delhi. I spent my early years there but at the age of six I was sent to a boarding preparatory school in England, down by the sea at Eastbourne. I don't remember objecting to this particularly. It was the usual pattern for the children of the British in India; the schooling facilities out there were extremely limited. My three elder brothers were all at boarding school and I took it for granted the same would happen to me.

I was luckier than some in that my headmaster was a humane type of man and realized that he had to try to take the place of absent fathers. On the other hand he believed in tough spirits and self-reliance. We were encouraged to take plenty of exercise and I can still recall the pleasure of walking across the Sussex downs without shoes or socks and feeling the short, springy grass beneath my bare feet.

When we were nearly due to go on to public school at the age of thirteen the head took a group of us on a cycling tour of France and towards the end of it left us to take ourselves back to England. He knew we could do it if we set our minds to the task and we had great fun finding our way to the ferry, crossing the Channel and riding back to Eastbourne. All in all, it was good training for youngsters and these early tests of initiative stood me in good stead later in life.

I went on to Bradfield College in Berkshire when I was thirteen and a half. I was reasonably good at class work but I lived for sport, particularly boxing, swimming and cross-country running. I liked to win. That feeling of pounding in ahead of everybody else is tremendous. I can still feel the thrill of it, even though my running days are long past.

The rebel in me began to come out at Bradfield and I was given six of the best time and time again. Another boy called Keats and myself found an ancient book in the back of an old cupboard one day. It was dated 1880 and contained about a couple of hundred school rules, everything from scrubbing our nails at night to keeping out of the masters' gardens. We set out to break each and every one of them and most of my thrashings came as a result of that. I didn't feel resentful about these canings. They were one of the hazards connected with school life and we regarded them as punishments for being caught rather than for committing a misdemeanour.

My bad behaviour must have reached something of a peak about two years after I went to Bradfield and at fifteen I was publicly beaten with a walking-stick in front of my house. This was almost without precedent and it had more effect on me than all the other beatings put together. I began to realize that I could not go on breaking all the rules all the time. It introduced a note of caution into my life and I was to appreciate later on that I had learned a valuable lesson.

While I was still at school all my brothers joined the Royal Engineers. I knew that I wanted to go into the Forces, where I thought I stood a much better chance of leading an adventurous life than by remaining a civilian. But at seventeen I decided to be contrary and volunteered for the Royal Navy. I was given time off from school to attend a medical examination in London. It was my first step alone into an authoritative establishment of the outside world and I was extremely nervous, but determined not to show it.

The medical was a strict one carried out by a doctor with a red beard assisted by various naval orderlies. He started at my head and worked down slowly to my feet while I stood tensed and alert, trying not to look embarrassed at my state of undress. I wanted to impress and obeyed sharply, and in what I hoped was a seamanlike manner, the various instructions which emerged from the beard.

After what must have been half an hour, though it seemed like half a day to me, the doctor reached my feet and prodded about at my toes. 'No sign of trouble there,' he muttered to an orderly who was standing by making notes for him.

I thought that was the end of it but apparently there were still the soles of my feet to examine and the doctor walked round behind me.

'Raise your right foot,' he grunted.

I snapped my leg back from the knee, sole upwards, determined to show that I was as wide awake at the end as I had been at the beginning. Unfortunately the doctor was not used to this barrack-square approach and, unknown to me, had knelt down to get a closer look at my foot. My smartly raised heel caught him smack on the nose.

Turning round, appalled at what I had done, I saw the doctor trying desperately to stem the flow of blood which was running down into his beard, making it redder still. One orderly was rushing up with a chair, another with a big roll of cotton wool. And it was then that I burst out laughing.

I suppose it was a nervous reaction after days of getting worked up about whether I would pass, followed by the actual ordeal of the examination itself. Anyway, I laughed, and it was such a relief that I had difficulty in stopping. Nobody else thought it was funny, or if they did they were not prepared to show their amusement in front of the injured doctor.

The upshot was, of course, that I didn't get into the Navy. The official reason given was that my feet were not up to standard; I have high arches. But I can't help feeling they would not have taken me at any price after my fit of the giggles.

After the first sharp disappointment I was not too depressed about this. I think I realized that I had volunteered in the first place just to be awkward, knowing that everyone expected me to follow my brothers into the Army.

I stayed on at Bradfield until I was eighteen, then won a place at the old Royal Military Academy at Woolwich, which was later absorbed into Sandhurst. It was a tough life but I enjoyed it. I remember I made friends mainly with the cadets from overseas, Australians, New Zealanders and Canadians. My parents were still abroad and could not get back to England very often, so the chaps from the Dominions and myself had in common the fact that we could not go home on leave like the others.

Tactics and strategy were my good subjects at the R.M.A. but I never won any prizes for smartness on parade. I am rather short and stocky, which isn't a good shape for the barrack square, and in any case my rebelliousness at the time was directed against what I considered to be excessive spit-and-polish. My objection to this remained throughout my army career. I maintain that a good soldier should be a trained fighting man, smart and proud of his appearance certainly, but not dressed up and bulled up like a tailor's dummy. I am glad to see that this is the attitude now being adopted throughout the Services.

I kept up with my sports at Woolwich, particularly boxing and swimming. I was put in for the pentathlon at the trials held to pick the British Olympics team. I got through at swimming, running and revolver shooting but I wasn't good enough at riding and épée fencing.

I passed out seventh in my year at the R.M.A. and went on to Cambridge University to study mechanical science, as I had decided after all that I wanted to follow my brothers into the Royal Engineers. The feeling that I needed to prepare myself for war was very strong in those days. I studied hard but I also went on with my sport to keep fit. I was awarded my half-blue for swimming and water polo and boxed for Cambridge and the Army, including a couple of fights at the Albert Hall.

Another step I took seems rather gruesome, looking back, but it played its part in my private preparation. I got a medical student friend to take me as often as possible into the medical school. There I could watch the students carving up bodies during their classes. My aim was to steel my mind to this type of thing so that I wouldn't be too shocked and sickened on the battlefield.

Of course, when it came to the point, the terrible and pathetic sights of war were far removed from the clinical and impersonal atmosphere of the medical school. But I felt that I was tougher, that my mind had been hardened; and the thought that I would no longer be quite as scared at seeing these things as I would have been without the surgical indoctrination helped a little, even though I was partly fooling myself.

It was 1936 when I won my honours degree and really started out as a Sapper officer; I had been commissioned before going to Cambridge. I was as proud as a peacock. I liked the life, there was plenty of time for sport and I was told I would be sent abroad very soon. A few months later I was on my way to Hong Kong and I felt that the adventurous life I had decided to lead was off to a good beginning.

2

My Coolie Army

The first men I commanded without let or hindrance in the British Army were Chinese coolies. I had set out in life deliberately seeking the unexpected but this was something I had never imagined, which made it entirely acceptable as far as I was concerned.

It happened in Hong Kong when, soon after I arrived, I was given the task of bringing up the strength of the Hong Kong Royal Engineers from 70 to 250. It was the sort of job many officers would treat with scorn, which is why it was handed to me as the junior subaltern. This never occurred to me at the time and I regarded it as a wonderful opportunity so early in my army career. And it really was a fine experience, as I had to plan a comprehensive programme which started with recruitment and went through all the training phases necessary to turn a raw recruit into a soldier. I was very much helped by a considerate Company Commander, Major Rollo Gillespie, and several others.

With my Chinese sergeant-major, named Yip Fuk, I selected the recruits from the Chinese volunteers. They flocked in when they heard there was a chance of joining the British Army and getting good pay and working conditions for several years if they were lucky enough to be accepted. I used to get up at six every morning and spend an hour studying Cantonese so that I could at least make an attempt to understand what my men were saying, and try to give them simple answers myself, instead of working all the time through an interpreter. I eventually passed an examination in Cantonese for which I received fifty pounds.

All the men had to have a trade before we signed them on and the majority of them took to army life at once. However hard they found the training I suppose they were living better than they had ever done,

15

or could ever hope to do, in their overcrowded homes. Their cheerful willingness made them easy to work with and patience and persuasion worked wonders. The respect they accorded me in return was heady stuff for a youngster and I remember shoving my head into the lion's mouth several times on their behalf.

Our local paymaster was a rather peppery major nearing retirement, the sort of officer that young subalterns normally tried to avoid. But I had to see him once or twice about general pay matters for the unit and when a special problem arose over one of my men I plucked up courage and asked for another interview.

'Well, what is it?' he barked, after I had saluted as if he was the Governor himself.

'It's about one of my men, sir.' I hesitated. The night before I had rehearsed exactly what to say and how to say it, brisk and to the point, but now I funked it and played for time. 'About . . . about his marriage allowance, sir.'

'Well, what about it, man? He gets one, doesn't he? If not there's a perfectly simple form you can fill in for him. Can't you write?'

'Yes, sir,' I said hastily. 'The trouble is . . . I was wondering . . . I mean, can a man have two marriage allowances?'

'*Two* marriage allowances!' The major turned red, then purple and for a moment seemed incapable of further speech.

I carried on quickly: 'You see, sir, one of my chaps has two wives and he finds it very difficult to keep them on one allowance, so I wondered if there was some special regulation . . .'

'Get out.' The major had found his tongue again but was using it with difficulty, judging from the strangled way he was speaking. 'If you think I have nothing better to do than worry about one of your over-sexed coolies then you must be more stupid than you look, which is difficult to believe.' He waved his hand in angry dismissal. 'I shall report this to your commanding officer.'

Luckily my C.O. was a different type altogether and in the end I managed to get the man with two wives some sort of extra pay, though it was not recorded as a double marriage allowance!

Pre-war Hong Kong had a fair smattering of awkward Regulars like the old paymaster, but there were plenty of really good officers too, the sort who considered their men's welfare first and their own last. They were firm disciplinarians but they were fair and even kindly, when kindness was needed, and the troops would have followed them anywhere. These were the men I tried to emulate and many of them went out of their way to help me along.

The Royal Scots were out there at the time and their colonel, who had given me some good advice in the past few months, invited me to sit in one morning when he was taking C.O.'s orders. I accepted like a shot and the hour and a half I spent there was worth more than all the man-management lectures I had ever had.

One of the men on a charge was a youngster of eighteen, not long out from Glasgow. The Royal Scots had been on Governor's sentry a few days before and this chap had relieved the monotony by taking pot shots with his rifle at passing cars carrying eminent visitors to the seat of Authority.

'Luckily for you, nobody was hurt,' the colonel told him when the official charge had been read out. 'Evidently you're not much of a shot. The reports show that not one of the cars was hit.' 'No, sir.' The young Scot was standing like a ram-rod, red-faced and staring straight in front of him.

'Well, what have you got to say?' the colonel demanded. 'This is a very serious charge and the Governor himself wants to know all about it.'

The Scot blinked at this and swallowed, without moving his head. 'Guilty, sorr',' he said.

The colonel slapped the papers on his desk angrily. 'We know that already,' he snapped. 'Yours was the only rifle that had been fired and you were short on your ammunition. What I want to know is *why* you did it. You had a good record at home and your N.C.O.s speak highly of you out here. Suddenly you take leave of your senses and start shooting at perfectly innocent people. Why?'

It was the typhoon season, the worst time of the year in Hong Kong just then, very hot and humid. My own shirt was sticking to my back and I saw the sweat begin to run down the young Scot's forehead. He was short and thick in build with a tough but pleasant-looking face which was now set and tensed under his glengarry. He was obviously scared stiff. He said nothing.

The colonel let him sweat for about half a minute then spoke again, more gently this time. 'Look, my lad, you're going to be punished anyway. You can't do an irresponsible thing like this and get away with it. But how can I decide your case fairly if you won't tell me why you did it? It's obvious to me that you're not the kind of idiot who would go around shooting at people just for the fun of it. But that's what everyone will think and you'll be landed with this sort of character for the rest of your time in the Army if you don't speak up.'

For a moment I thought this excellent piece of commonsense persuasion was going to have no effect, but then the boy's eyes wavered and the tip of his tongue came out to moisten his lips.

'Y'see, sorr, it was so hot and . . . and I was —ing brooned Off, sorr!' he burst out.

It was the first time I had heard the expression 'browned off' but it was obviously not new to the colonel.

'We all get fed up at times,' he said severely, 'but the world would be a dreadful place if we all did damn' silly things like this when we felt out of sorts.' He paused. 'However, the heat out here at this time of the year can be tough, even on the old hands. We'll get the M.O. to have a look at you. Meanwhile you've got to pay for your stupidity.'

The colonel gave the boy twenty-eight days' detention, although it was a case which could easily have gone to a court martial and landed him in a military jail for two or three years.

'What good would he have been when he came out?' the colonel said when I mentioned this to him later on. 'I know these young Scots. Some of them are too wild to hold but I'm ready to bet that one will make a good soldier.'

He spoke with complete confidence and I knew that his assessment was based on years of acting not only as judge and jury but also as mother and father and wet nurse to more men than he would care to remember. It never occurred to me to question his judgement; I could only hope that one day my own would be as sure.

Later on in the Far East I was lucky enough to get a copybook example of how to get the best out of a man by giving him confidence and a feeling of responsibility, instead of slapping him down and making him more resentful than ever, as so often happened.

My 'tutor' this time was Colonel Barchard of the Royal Welch Fusiliers, a fine officer who was really loved by his men. But they were a tough crowd with a liking for living it up occasionally and there was one man in particular who was always landing himself in a mess.

He was known as '47 Jones, '47 being the last two figures in his army number, and he was a really good welterweight boxer and rugger player. The trouble was he could never confine his fighting to the ring and after a good night out he invariably got mixed up in a scrap just for the hell of it.

I was in Colonel Barchard's office one day when '47 Jones came up on yet another charge. This time he had laid out three military policemen.

'Now look, Jones, there's got to be an end to this,' the colonel said severely.

'Yes, sir.'

'It's no good just saying "Yes, sir". That's what you say every time. I give you twenty-eight days' and as soon as you finish that you're back here again. Something has got to be done to stop it.'

'Yes, Sir.'

The colonel looked at him grimly. 'I should have you court martialled as an incurable troublemaker. But I'll give you one more chance. Are you willing to accept my award?'

'47 Jones, whose big frame had stiffened at the mention of a court martial, managed to look relieved without moving a muscle of his rather battered face as he stood to attention.

'Sir.'

'Right,' said Colonel Barchard. 'From now on you'll be my batman. I'm always getting into trouble myself and it'll be your job to keep me out of it.'

'Yes, Sir.'

In many other units '47 Jones would have been court martialled long before the escapade I have recalled, and the Army would have lost a good soldier. As far as I know he was never in serious trouble again, although Colonel Barchard told me when we met later that he sometimes imposed unofficial 'confined to barracks' sentences on Jones. The sole object of this was to make sure he got himself fit before a boxing match!

I learned much about my profession from these colonels and other officers of the same type who were ready to throw the rule book out of the window when their judgement told them it was wrong. I tried to put into practice the methods they used. Getting to know men who are naturally suspicious because of the pips on your shoulder is hard work. As in everything else, there are times when it just doesn't work out and that can be depressing. But at the other end of the scale an officer gets a tremendous feeling of satisfaction and pride in knowing that he has the confidence and loyalty of the men serving under him.

I like to think that this was the case with my Hong Kong Royal Engineers. Before I left them in 1937 to go to Shanghai they had beaten a number of British units at soccer and water polo and had been given the place of honour in a big march-past in Hong Kong, leading all the Royal Engineer units serving in the colony at that time. I was sorry to leave them but I knew I was handing over a going concern to my successor and I was pleased that my first real job in the Army had turned out so well.

A few years later these men fought valiantly in the defence of Hong Kong and when it eventually fell to the Japs many of them escaped and trekked thousands of miles across occupied China into India, so that they could carry on fighting. But nobody knew quite what to do with them and they were left kicking their heels in a transit camp at Deolali, near Bombay.

I happened to visit the camp while preparing for the 1944 Wingate campaign into Burma and suddenly saw some familiar-looking Chinese faces. We had a joyful reunion and they told me how they came to be there. They were being well looked after but it was clear they felt they were not wanted, despite the hardships they had suffered for the chance to fight again.

There were about 100 of them all told. I knew quite a few because I had recruited them, and the others had either joined after I left Hong Kong or came from other volunteer units in the colony. They all had battle experience against the Japs and were very fit after their hard trek followed by a rest in the camp. They were the sort of men I wanted in Burma and I asked them if they would join me again to fight in the jungle.

I didn't have to ask twice and soon after that they were with the rest of my brigade in training. So my coolies became Chindits and when I saw them fight I knew that my pride in them in 1937 had not been misplaced.

3

Blooded in Shanghai

I was looking for excitement and adventure when I decided to join the Army and in 1937 there was no better place to find this than Shanghai.

About half the trade of China went through this great port and for many years it had been a bustling centre of operations for wealthy merchants from Europe and America. The white business men and their families lived mainly in the British, French and American quarters. These areas of the crowded city had been ceded to the Western countries by the Chinese Government, and their white inhabitants were entitled to be protected by their own forces. When I went from Hong Kong to join the British garrison in Shanghai the need for this protection was only too apparent.

Following their conquest of Manchuria in the early 'thirties the aggressive Japanese had crossed the border and taken over several provinces in north-eastern China. They had even set up a puppet government in Peking. Not satisfied with this, they were soon on the move again and by July, 1937, the Sino-Japanese War was really on. It did not take a great military mind to work out that Shanghai, with its tremendous port facilities and strategic coastal position, would be high on the list of Japanese targets.

Of course, the Western countries were not involved in the war and it was considered that the Japs would try to avoid trouble by keeping their troops outside Shanghai's International Settlement. On the other hand it would be just about impossible for Chinese and Jap troops fighting furiously in the town and its surrounds to keep strictly within certain boundaries. The job of pointing out that they had strayed would certainly be a dangerous and tricky one, and there would also be the chance of damage and casualties from bullets, bombs and shells landing off-target.

In fact several British soldiers were killed by stray shells and this caused quite a lot of feeling both in Shanghai and at home in London.

Although we were not directly concerned in the conflict our politicians and top strategists clearly had in mind the possibility of a war against the Japs at some future date. The followers of the Rising Sun were beginning to regard themselves as invincible conquerors and if this mood continued, as all the signs suggested it would, it could only be a question of time before their thoughts turned to parts of the Far East and Pacific area under our control. We would then have to stop them and the sooner we began to learn how they fought, the better equipped we would be when the time came.

That was the theory and in my view it was an excellent one; there is no wiser motto than Be Prepared. In Shanghai we did our best to put that theory into practice but, all too often, valuable information obtained at great risk in the midst of some of the fiercest fighting I have ever seen was pigeonholed or just ignored by blasé staff officers sitting in the War Office in London. If this information had been considered and acted upon our forces might not have been in such a poor state in 1939.

I can give one instance of this appalling negligence from my own experience.

Because I could speak Cantonese I was chosen on occasions to go out with the Chinese forces as an observer. I did not realize it at the time but, looking back, I consider that was when World War II started for me. I saw as much fighting in the few months that the Shanghai battle lasted as I saw throughout the rest of my army career. It was a continuous and bloody struggle between two enemies with a plentiful supply of the main essential for a land battle: troops. The number of casualties was fantastic. The Japs lost about 200,000 men and the Chinese a great deal more than that. As a baptism of fire the slaughter of Shanghai was all that the hungriest adventure-seeker could want and a lot more besides.

I also learned much about the Japs that stood me in good stead later on in Burma. Not the least of the lessons was that a well trained Japanese soldier was a man to be reckoned with – cunning, tenacious and often very brave. I have made my share of mistakes, and probably more, but after Shanghai I never made the fatal error of underestimating the Japs; too many men who did are now dead.

22

Although the Chinese did not mind our going with them to watch the fighting they could obviously give no guarantee of safety, so we made our own arrangements to try to keep hidden. One of my disguises was as a sack of potatoes in a bullock cart; the driver could pick up more money in a few hours carrying one or two crazy Britons about than he normally earned in a month. For him, the risks were well worth while.

It was from a bullock cart that I watched the Japanese invade Hangchow Bay, using a fleet of boats of a type that I had never seen before. They appeared to be flat-bottomed, because they could get almost out of the water on to the beach. Their sides were high and presumably armour-plated or protected from bullets in some other way. But the most interesting point of all was that, when they could get no nearer the shore, their flat bows opened downwards like a drawbridge over a moat and the troops poured out of them on to the beaches.

These were landing craft, and as far as I knew the British Army had nothing like them. The Japanese took them close inshore in a whaling ship, then dropped them from the stern; their value was obvious and I could hardly contain myself. I wanted to leap out from my protective covering of smelly sacks and run all the way back to camp to tell my superiors what I had seen. As it was I stayed watching these marvellous new craft and made copious notes about how they worked, how many troops they carried and so on. My report on this outing would make the staff boys sit up!

There was plenty of enthusiastic reaction among my immediate superiors in Shanghai and my report went through to Major-General Telfer-Smollet, the Shanghai area Commander. I was told that he had sent it on to London and we waited for the reaction; perhaps there would be a request for more information or for clarification on one or two points. We heard nothing, but we took the hopeful view that the report had been so clear that the War Office were able to act on it without further reference to us.

In fact that was the last I heard about landing craft until three years later, after the war had started. We were beginning to build them then, but for another year or two they were in short supply. We could so easily have been well stocked if a few staff officers had taken more interest in 1937.

This is just one small example of the sort of mistakes that nearly cost us our freedom in 1939 and 1940, when we had the men, the spirit and the will to fight, but virtually no equipment for them to use.

In between my observation patrols I carried on with my normal duties as an engineer. One of the jobs assigned to the Sappers was dealing with the fairly large number of unexploded bombs and shells that were falling in the International Settlement. Unfortunately, during my training I had either missed or skipped most of the lectures and demonstrations on this subject. But I did not like to confess this and decided to rely on improvisation.

I had been told there were no time fuses on the bombs so it was obvious that they, like the shells, were just duds that should have exploded on impact but had some fault. I worked on the theory that if they had not gone off after crashing to the ground there must be something pretty badly wrong with them and they were therefore safe enough to move.

A canal known as the Soo Chow Creek runs through the centre of Shanghai and this seemed to be the perfect dumping place for dud explosives. I had been given a platoon of the Royal Welch Fusiliers to help clear the area and after tossing a few shells and bombs into the creek myself without incident, I told them to help me pick up the rest and load them into several carts that I had borrowed from some coolies. The fusiliers seemed a little worried about this so to reassure them I said it was quite safe as long as they held the shells and bombs horizontally.

Looking back I shudder to think what might have happened if one of those 'duds' had gone off; but my luck held good and we heaved all we could find into the creek and no one was any the worse. They must have been badly made and probably the risk was not as great as it sounds. I like to think that, anyway.

We had some fun, too, in Shanghai. I was still boxing and there were various sporting events between the different garrisons in the area. On one of these occasions I was matched in a six-round fight against an American Marine who had beaten all his opponents in places like Hawaii and the Philippines and was called 'The Champ of the Pacific'.

We were friendly enough with the Americans but their well-known cock-sureness and general inclination to do a bit of showing-off at every opportunity sometimes riled the more stolid British troops. So feelings began to run rather high several days before the fight when the Americans were betting ten to one that their 'champ' would beat hell out of the Limey officer who was stupid enough to get into the ring with him. The British troops, for their part, were taking the bets and offering ten to one that I would beat the Marine. I think they were afraid I *would* get the stuffing knocked out of me but they were damned if they were going to admit it!

With all this going on the atmosphere was pretty electric on the night of the fight. The hall where it was being held was packed with British and American troops and there were occasional outbreaks of partisan shouting and general ribaldry.

My second was an Australian physical training instructor, a grand chap called Snowy White. He thought I could beat the American but he was a cautious type and decided he would like to know what was going on over in the opposition corner. He worked out a plan and on the big night brought his ten-year-old son with him to the hall; he shoved him under the ring before the fight started with instructions to creep over and listen in to the 'champ' and his seconds and report back to Dad. In fact I don't think this made any difference to the outcome but Snowy felt happier with this regular flow of information and the youngster certainly enjoyed himself.

The fight itself turned out to be not as difficult as I thought it would be. The Marine was a tough chap and a good boxer and he gave me some nasty knocks in the first couple of rounds. But I was fitter than he was and I kept him on the go to tire him before moving in myself.

The Americans had been cheering like mad in the early stages but gradually they quietened down and the British troops took over to cheer me on as I began to get the upper hand. I heard afterwards that the Marine was used to winning by a quick knock-out and had not reckoned on more than a round or two. Whatever the reason, he was losing ground fast by the fourth round and I was giving him a hammering.

Some of the Americans began to sidle out of the hall when the fifth round started and my supporters jeered derisively at this. 'Had enough, Yank? Where are you going, Yank?' were two of the more printable expressions I heard vaguely from the ring.

I knocked out the 'champ' before the end of the round and the troops went crazy. There was not much in the way of entertainment for them and this was one of the few ways they could let off steam. The rivalry between the different units did no harm and gave them something to think about. There was good co-operation in the serious things that mattered and I would have been very happy to have the 'champ' and some of his Marine friends alongside me in a scrap.

All this time the fighting was going on not only in and around Shanghai but also out on the Great Plain of China. The Japs, of course, knew that we were collecting as much information as possible from the battle for future use. From time to time they captured one or two Britons but normally they were content to make life uncomfortable for them for a few days and lodge official protests before releasing them.

I was taken prisoner once on an observation trip with a civilian engineer called Whitehouse, who spoke Japanese. A Jap patrol marched us off to their local headquarters with revolvers pressed to our backs, so there was no chance of escape.

It looked like the same routine, with the Japs making themselves generally unpleasant and putting on a big show before releasing us. My main feeling was one of annoyance at having been careless enough to allow myself to be captured in the first place. I was also wondering what would happen if the Japs played their little trick of stripping British prisoners in an attempt to humiliate them. I had heard about this in Shanghai and now wore underpants with the Rising Sun sewn on the back! Perhaps I would soon know how the Japs reacted to this insult to their national flag.

At the headquarters we were pushed into the guardroom and locked up. No one seemed very interested in us; and our protests at being treated like enemies, when we were, of course, peaceable neutrals, were brushed aside. This puzzled us, for we had expected violent accusations that we had been spying on Japanese forces.

As we sat in our cell we became increasingly conscious of a crowd of people shouting and singing somewhere nearby. We decided it must be coming from elsewhere in the camp; and soon afterwards we heard our own guards laughing and joking in the main guardroom. Whitehouse said he would find out what was going on and yelled in Japanese until one of the sentries came to see what he wanted. Far from being annoyed at us the Jap stood in the passage and grinned amiably through the iron grille.

'Who's doing all the singing?' Whitehouse asked, nodding at the barred and glassless window; the noise coming through it was now louder than ever.

The Jap's grin widened and I noticed that he seemed rather unsteady on his feet. 'We're all celebrating,' he said happily. 'We've driven your friends the Chinese out of Nanking.' He went on gabbling away and Whitehouse said the gist of it was that this was also the Japanese New Year which made it a double celebration.

After the guard had gone back to join his pals Whitehouse said that, from what he knew of the Japs, the roistering would go on for some time yet and he reckoned we should take advantage of it.

'That's all very well', I said, 'and I'm game to try anything. But we're still locked up in this cell with a crowd of Japs hanging around drinking just outside. I imagine drunk Japs are just as likely to shoot us down as sober Japs, probably more so.'

Whitehouse grinned. 'I wasn't thinking of trying to bust the door down and making a run for it. I'm going to try and talk us out. We'll probably get a thick ear or two delivered by rifle butt if it doesn't work, but I think it's worth a try. Are you on?'

I agreed at once and while we waited for an hour or so to give the liquor plenty of chance to do its work Whitehouse sketched out his scheme, which was only possible because of his excellent command of Japanese.

At the time we had fixed he went to the door and began yelling again for the Jap guard. At first we thought the whole lot were incapable of walking, for no one answered. But eventually our old friend came staggering up and by this time he was well away. Almost before Whitehouse could say a word to him he slipped to the floor and passed out.

Whitehouse really got going then, bawling his head off about 'disgraceful conduct', and soon a young Jap lieutenant came along. He must either have been a conscientious duty officer or a teetotaller, because he was as sober as we were. But he looked pretty harassed and I almost felt sorry for him; being in charge at that camp on that particular night must have been quite a job.

'What is the meaning of this disgusting behaviour?' Whitehouse demanded severely. 'Look at this man on the floor. Dead drunk. And from the sound of it the rest of the men are nearly as bad. Is this the way the Japanese Army behaves?'

On a normal night he would never have got away with it. As it was, the lieutenant made a half-hearted attempt to brazen it out.

'What concern is it of yours?' He tried to sound haughty. 'You are merely prisoners.'

This gave Whitehouse the lead he wanted. 'You know perfectly well that you can't keep us here for long,' he said. 'And as soon as we get back to Shanghai an official complaint will go through at the highest level to your government representatives.'

Whitehouse paused to let this sink in. 'A fine piece of reading it will make, as well,' he added. ' "Officers and men of His Imperial Majesty's Army drunk on duty while guarding British prisoners." I wonder what they'll say in Tokyo.'

The lieutenant crumpled at this and before Whitehouse had finished was practically begging him not to report what we had seen and heard. Whitehouse said we might be able to forget it if we were released immediately and provided with an escort back to Shanghai, as a safeguard against being picked up by another Jap patrol. The lieutenant checked and discovered that our arrest had not yet been reported to any higher command, as would have happened on a normal day. So if we were released there would be no awkward questions from above.

It was not long before we were on our way back to Shanghai, escorted by half a dozen men who had recently returned from patrol and had not yet had time to drink themselves senseless. Without Whitehouse I could have been in a really tight spot. If a few drunk Japs had decided to bait the British prisoners that night and discovered the Rising Sun on my pants I hate to think what might have happened.

Soon after this escapade the Japs overcame the Chinese opposition in the whole of the Shanghai area and occupied part of the city, while still respecting the International Settlement boundaries. For the British troops Shanghai became more or less a normal garrison job once again, though fighting was still going on in other parts of China and the situation was far from settled.

Later on in 1938 I returned home. My first tour abroad had been a wonderful experience and I found the East fascinating. The thought that I would almost certainly be going back one day made leaving it a little easier. There was also the fact that what newspapers call the 'crisis flashpoint' was now in the West, and I wanted to be there if action was on the cards.

The tension was fairly high. All over Europe diplomats and politicians were meeting and talking and bargaining and shaking hands in front of photographers; it all seemed very ominous. To many of us, the warnings about German rearmament that people like Winston Churchill had been giving over the past few years began to look fully justified. On the other hand, a lot of people were still doubtful whether Hitler would take on the Allies, and the now notorious policy of appeasement was in full swing.

As far as the Services were concerned, we had to try to be ready in case the worst happened. The trouble was that too little had been done in the years before. While Hitler had built up his power ours had been allowed to run down, and there was little time left to repair the damage. The inevitable result was that, when the war came, we were still far from ready for it, and paid the price of unpreparedness with defeat after defeat.

4

The 'Phoney Fifth'

For some months before the war started I was adjutant of the London Divisional Engineers with the temporary rank of captain. I had never worked so hard before and hoped fervently that I would never have to do so again. As the situation worsened the work got tougher and after war was declared on September 3rd, 1939, the heat was really on.

We doubled, trebled and quadrupled our numbers, calling the men in, equipping them, training the recruits and retraining the reserves. As adjutant I was in the thick of it and I began to realize what it must be like running a mass-production factory at full capacity with grasping customers waiting at the doors. Our production line never stopped. The men came in at one end from Civvy Street and went off the other end on to a boat to France just as fast as we could turn them out.

The pressure was terrific and for a time I was so caught up in the job that I had time to think of little else. I bought a car when I came back from the East so that I could enjoy myself taking trips at weekends. I hardly ever used it. The weeks went by and vaguely I was aware of an uneasiness at the back of my mind, but there was too little time to work out what it was. Then, at the end of November, Russia created a diversion by attacking Finland. For some time the Moscow Reds had been worried about their north-western borders in case of an attack from that quarter. But the Finns stuck to their independence and refused various pacts and agreements suggested by the Soviet Union. Finally the Russians demanded the use of several ports on the Finnish coast as naval bases for the Red Fleet in the Baltic. Again Finland refused. And this time the men in the Kremlin decided to take what they wanted by force.[1]

To everyone's surprise the Reds were thrown back. And the brave stand made by the Finns as they beat off the Soviet troops in a series of running fights across the frontier snows captured the headlines for a while. In Western Europe World War II had not really got under way; it was the period which became known as the Phoney War. But there was nothing phoney about the fierce battles in Finland.

I followed the news with great interest in London whenever I could snatch a moment or two from my administrative chores. The amount of paper work I had to get through was sometimes almost overwhelming. All the official bumf from the War Office and other departments came through me as adjutant and I was getting sick of the sight of it. Much of it I could hardly bear to read, but one day in December I spotted something that riveted my attention: it was a request for volunteers to go out and help the Finns.

Suddenly I knew what it was that had been worrying me. I had been flogging myself to a standstill at home working like a recruiting and training machine, then sending the finished product to France. I was told I was doing too valuable a job to be sent myself and for a while I had fallen for the flattery. But I wanted to fight. That was the fretful thought nagging at the back of my mind. I had had my dose of paper-and-desk work, now what I craved for was action.

I studied the call for volunteers more carefully. They would automatically join the Scots Guards, who were forming a special ski battalion, the 5th, to go to Finland. Volunteers of all ranks would revert to private; and no guarantees were being issued that old ranks would be regained if and when they came back.

I thought for a while about this. The Army was my career, I had spent the last eight years either training to be an officer or serving as one. Should I throw all this away? It did not take me long to decide that I should; this was no time to consider careers. In any case I was getting near the end of my tether with the training job. I wasn't made

[1] On 30th November 1939 Soviet warships began bombarding Finnish ports and Helsinki suffered the first of several air raids aimed at the civilian population. Half a million Soviet troops crossed the border, greatly outnumbering the 130,000 defenders. The well trained Finns put up a magnificent fight and by the end of December had destroyed two Soviet divisions.

to sit behind a desk or strut around a barrack square. There was a war on and I wanted to fight and if the only way to do it was to become a private, then a private I would be.

A further point in the circular was that commanding officers would not be able to stop their men volunteering. I heard afterwards that the thought behind this was that obviously the sort of man who would be mad enough to put in for Finland would probably be the sort most C.O.s would want to keep in wartime. Anyway, that clinched it for me. I would be unpopular with my superiors, but what did that matter? They would have to let me go.

It would be difficult to imagine a more unlikely lot of Guardsmen than the 5th Scots Guards, who reported for duty at Bordon Barracks in Hampshire. We were all shapes and sizes (I was several inches under Guards regulation height) and we came from a variety of different units. Some had even volunteered straight from Civvy Street and several had been fighting in recent years wherever they could find a war – places like Spain, China and South America.

Despite all this, or perhaps because of it, I have rarely served with a grander bunch of chaps and I suppose it was inevitable that later on many of them would play leading parts in the various special forces, such as the Commandos, Special Air Service, Long Range Desert Group, Chindits, etc.

A volunteer many of us were amazed to see at Bordon was one of the Rothschilds, the wealthy Jewish banking family. If anybody could have bought himself a safe job he could, but here he was on what was potentially a suicide mission. We began roughing it at once; for instance, cold water to shave in, not hot. And I remember wondering how many times this had happened before to a Rothschild! But there were no complaints from this one, who still seemed quite happy. And he took it cheerfully enough when he drew the job of latrine orderly. He had to get up early for this and I shall never forget his polite question in a dark and freezing-cold barrack room at 5.30 one morning: 'Excuse me, has any gentleman seen the latrine superintendent's broom?' He also had to borrow a tape measure, because Bordon discipline was Guards discipline and each window in the latrine had to be opened the same number of inches as the rest! When I heard years later that Rothschild had done some courageous work for the French Resistance I was not surprised; he was made of the right stuff.

We appreciated that outwardly we had to stick to Guards discipline, but off duty rank meant very little to us. Although I was made a platoon sergeant I refused to draw up a roster for the various odd jobs that had to be done. I just listed the tasks and the men played dice to decide who did them. For a bunch of individuals on this type of mission it was the best way.

After a week or two at Bordon we went out to Chamonix, near the Swiss-French border, for ski training with the crack French ski troops, the Chasseurs Alpine. We spent a hectic time climbing mountains and rushing down them again on skis, and it wasn't until some time afterwards that I discovered the land we were supposed to fight over in Finland was dead flat. Presumably the need to get us ready and away was so urgent that no one had enquired what sort of country we would find out there; they knew we had to ski and obviously that meant training on ski slopes. I suppose it was a fair enough assumption and in any case it got us used to wearing the things, although personally I never got on well with them.

About six weeks after we had first gathered at Bordon we were told that our rough-and-ready training was finished and we were on our way to Finland. We travelled back to England from Chamonix and on up to Gareloch, on the Clyde, where we embarked on the Polish liner *Batory*. It was early March, 1940, and I was glad to think that before long I would be in action again. Shanghai seemed far away.

Then, just before we sailed, news came through that the Finns had been beaten and their three-month struggle was over. They had done wonders in holding back the mighty Red Army for so long, but they never really stood a chance. The Russians underestimated them to begin with and used inferior troops and the wrong tactics. But they quickly learned their lesson, brought up fresh and highly-trained men and got down to the job in earnest. The end was inevitable.[2]

But it was a terrible anticlimax for us and we cursed the authorities for not letting us go straight out there when we had first volunteered instead of spending what turned out to be vital weeks on a training

---

[2] Allied intervention would have been very difficult, with neutral Sweden refusing to allow foreign troops to cross its soil. On 15th March, the Finnish 'Diet' ratified the Moscow peace agreement. Almost half a million civilians, one eighth of the population, began to leave the areas taken over by the Russians.

course which had really been pretty useless anyway. However, we were talking with hindsight and it is clear now that we would have made little difference to the Red Army's victory even if we had reached Finland in time to fight.

My own feeling of disappointment soon turned to abject misery. I had been unwell for several days and after a night sleeping too near an open porthole on the *Batory* I was sent ashore to hospital with pneumonia. A fine end to what had promised to be an exciting and satisfying mission!

The hospital I landed in was a ghastly place and I got out of it as fast as I could. As with so many things at that confused time early in the war, no one seemed to know whether the place was being run by civilians or the military. The staff was a mixture of both and they were certainly not very interested in me. As soon as I felt strong enough to move under my own steam, I insisted on my discharge. By this time, of course, the rest of the 5th Scots Guards had disembarked from the *Batory* and returned to London. I caught the first available train and followed them.

At Wellington Barracks, the Guards headquarters near Buckingham Palace, I was eyed with great suspicion as I marched up to the orderly room; a Scots Guards sergeant of my height was an unusual spectacle there, to say the least. In the orderly room I explained my position to a company sergeant-major.

'5th Scots Guards?' he barked, looking even more suspicious than the other Guardsmen I had passed. 'They've been disbanded. Didn't you know that?'

'I've been in hospital,' I explained, wondering what on earth I was supposed to do now. 'They were still on the *Batory* when I last saw them.'

I gave the C.S.M. my full name and number. He checked up and became a little more friendly when it appeared I wasn't an impostor.

'The "Phoney Fifth", we call 'em,' he said, cracking a brief and wintry smile. 'Didn't last long, did they?'

'What do I do now?' I asked. The last thing I felt like was joking. 'I haven't been disbanded but my unit has. Where does that leave me?'

'God knows.' The C.S.M. began shuffling the papers on his desk as if anxious to get back to work. 'The only thing I can tell you is that you're not in the Scots Guards any longer.' The thought seemed to please him.

I was at a complete loss and must have looked it, for the C.S.M. took pity on me for a moment. 'Where were you before you joined the phoneys?' he demanded.

'London Divisional Engineers,' I replied automatically.

'I'd go back to them if I were you,' he said. 'There's nothing for you here.'

After the way I had left them I did not imagine the London Divisional Engineers would welcome me back with open arms, and as I wandered off down Birdcage Walk I felt so low that I nearly cried; I was still weak after my illness and the shock of suddenly finding myself on my own, with no unit and perhaps even out of the Army, was almost too much to bear.

Luckily I have a fairly cheerful nature and soon the ridiculousness of the whole situation began to arouse my sense of humour. Was I Captain Calvert of the Royal Engineers, or Sergeant Calvert of the Scots Guards, or Mr. Calvert, unemployed, of no fixed address? I hadn't the faintest idea and thinking about it made me giddy, so I decided to shelve the problem until the morning and enjoy myself. One advantage of not being sure what you are is that you are not so particular about what you do.

At that time London seemed somewhat like me: not quite sure what it was supposed to be. There was a mixed air of uncertainty and expectancy hanging about the streets and buildings; the solid atmosphere of a peaceful and powerful capital had vanished, but as yet there was nothing to replace it. Later on, of course, when the bombs began to fall, it reasserted its strong character and became the tough, courageous centre of the struggle against Hitler. Early in 1940, however, London was still in the difficult transitional period between war and peace, and so were many of the people in it.

Late that night I found myself sitting alone at a table in the Café de Paris, still in my Scots Guards uniform. A boisterous crowd at a nearby table waved cheerily and invited me to join them.

'You're rather short for a Guardsman, old boy,' said one of the men, who was in R.A.F. officer's uniform.

I had had a few drinks by then so I drew myself up and announced

35

solemnly: 'I'll have you know that I'm the last surviving member of the 5th Scots Guards.'

They cheered and someone insisted on ordering champagne to celebrate my survival. By the time I fell into my bed in the Union Jack Club near Waterloo Station I no longer cared who or what I was!

No leave had come my way for several months and the next morning I decided it would be as well to have some and work out my next move when I felt better. It was a Sunday and it seemed a fair bet that the British weekend would still be in force at Wellington Barracks. Sure enough the senior N.C.O. in the orderly room was a corporal, who was quite prepared to accept my story that I was going on disbanding leave and needed a pass and a railway warrant for the orderly officer to sign.

I left the barracks and made out the pass to Sergeant Calvert, J.M., 584321. Then I signed it J. M. Calvert, Captain, Royal Engineers. After repeating the process with the railway warrant I went off to Devonshire, where my parents were then living in retirement.

A fortnight in the country put me right again and I returned to London fighting fit and determined to get back into the Army even if it meant volunteering at a recruiting centre.

However, I was keeping that as a last resort and began by reporting to the War Office. It appeared they had been wondering what had happened to me since the 5th Scots Guards packed up. In the general shambles no one had reported my illness and I had apparently vanished.

'We decided to wait for a bit to see if you turned up,' one of the staff captains said. 'Your old C.O. told us you weren't the sort to get lost.'

In the end, as so often happens, it was all much easier than I had thought it would be. Although I had resigned my commission the Finnish business had been such a mix-up, and so short-lived, that they were prepared to forget it ever happened and I got my commission back.

We were now well into April and the whole war situation looked grim, to say the least. The Germans were rolling across Europe and there was nothing the under-equipped and under-trained Allied troops could do to stop them. The picture was much the same in Norway, where the Germans had made successful landings and were rapidly overrunning the country.[3]

Plans were being made to land a British Expeditionary Force and other Allied troops at various points along the west coast of Norway, from Narvik in the north to Andalsnes in the south, in a series of desperate attempts to stop the Germans. I had been training to fight in the snow and there was plenty of it in Norway, as well as in Finland, so I asked the War Office if I could go on one of these landings. They agreed.

I was posted as adjutant to a Royal Engineers unit going in with the B.E.F. to a place called Andalsnes. There were no last-minute hitches on this trip; the ship sailed and I stayed in rude health. And within a few days I was at last in action, for the first time in World War II proper.

---

[3] On 9th April the German cruiser 'Blucher' led a troop convoy into Oslo harbour. It was promptly sunk by torpedoes from Fort Oscarsborg but the assault continued and the 163rd Infantry Division and a battalion of paratroopers finally captured the capital as the German fleet landed troops at six other Norwegian ports. The small army tried to block the valleys and prevent the enemy forces in Oslo linking up with those landed on the coast. However, the élite German 169th Mountain Division began to outflank the Norwegian blocks, which soon came under attack by dive bombing Stukas.

5

Avalanche!

Within a few days of our arrival in Norway it became clear that our mission was doomed to failure almost before it had begun. The aim was to carry out a pincer movement on the big port of Trondheim and part of the British Expeditionary Force landed to the north, at Namsos, and the rest to the south, at Andalsnes. Each group advanced inland with the intention of circling round to meet at Trondheim. But by this time the Germans were nearing the western coast in much greater strength than expected and the B.E.F.'s task appeared to be a hopeless one.

Andalsnes was a small fishing port at the head of Romsdal Fiord and the infantry's first objective was Dombas, about seventy miles away at the other end of the Romsdal Gorge. We stayed behind and set about forming a base depot at Andalsnes, although there had been precious few supplies available to bring with us. Meanwhile the attacking force reached Dombas and pressed on even further, but soon news of strong enemy opposition filtered through and we began to realize that there would be little need for the normal base services on this trip. So my C.O. sent me off along the Romsdal Gorge in the wake of the infantry to reconnoitre the area and decide where demolitions could cause the enemy most harm.

I set off on a motor-cycle with a sergeant, roaring through the snow-covered countryside in the direction of Dombas. The aim of the demolitions was to slow down the German advance and give our men more time to get away. Our main objectives were therefore roads, the railway that ran along the gorge, and bridges. Despite the depressing thought that we were having to get out so soon I found it exhilarating, in the crisp Norwegian air, to be on the point of some positive action at last.

We spent two or three days selecting demolition points along the Romsdal Gorge and then a Sapper sergeant-major who had collected a group of 'volunteers' brought up our explosives from Andalsnes in a truck. I found that the only explosives available were sea mines and depth charges. The mines were of a type I had not come across before and this was my first acquaintance with depth charges, which are normally strictly naval weapons. However, as my sergeant pointed out, they certainly contained explosives and as long as we could find the right way to set the stuff off there seemed no reason why they shouldn't blow up roads and bridges just as well as they blew up submarines. We then discovered that there was no electrical equipment, which meant using matches applied directly to a safety fuse. Finally, just to prove that misfortunes come in threes, the amount of fuse available made the word 'safety' almost meaningless.

For a couple of days the 'volunteers', mostly young artillery chaps whose guns had come over in a different ship and were now at the bottom of the North Sea, helped us get the heavy mines and depth charges into position at the points I had chosen. My orders were to wait until I saw the whites of the enemy's eyes; in other words to set off the explosives as near as possible to when the Germans arrived at each selected point. So the working party humped and heaved the weighty containers into position and left them there. Later the sergeant and I would return alone to set them off.

The working party then went back to Andalsnes and by this time the infantry were beginning to pass through us on their way out. We gathered that the spearhead of the German advance was now in the area of Dombas but had been slowed down by the snow and supply and communication difficulties. However, enemy air activity was beginning to be a nuisance. Figures on the ground show up very well against a white background of snow and we soon found that German fighter pilots were only too happy to use us for target practice with their machine-guns.

We had made our headquarters in a hillside bungalow which gave the appearance of having been evacuated pretty swiftly by its owners. There was a stove and a certain amount of fuel, which was a great comfort in the intense cold. Sometimes we felt quite alone up there in the snow, but then we would go out to check some of our charges and a German fighter would spot us. All too soon we would realize we were far from alone in that crisp white world and the machine-gun bullets would kick up the snow too near for comfort as we hid in rock crevices or any other fold or dip in the ground that we could find. Often we fired back at the fighters with our rifles, without much effect, but it helped our morale.

Finally it was time to start setting off our explosives and a platoon of Marines came up to act as a covering party while the sergeant and I fixed the fuses. On one occasion we timed things a little too nicely and two lorry-loads of Germans arrived unexpectedly before we had finished the job. There was quite a fight and a young Marine subaltern named Stroud did a wonderful job holding the Germans at bay while I went on with the demolition. Later, on my recommendation, Stroud was awarded the Military Cross.

Soon after that the Marines were called back and although this meant we were rather more exposed and had to keep watch ourselves as well as lighting our explosives, in practice it was a better proposition. Because of the nearness of the Germans and the shortage of fuse a quick getaway from the point of explosion was essential. The sergeant and I could do our job then race off, sliding and skidding our way to safety on the motor-cycle, without having to worry about the Marines.

Another good reason for getting away as fast as possible was the fact that our explosions were liable to cause avalanches, in the surrounding hills as the blast echoed round. This had not occurred to us until we let off our first big bang and were nearly buried beneath tons of snow hurtling down on to the road where our charges had exploded. It was a really frightening experience and I never knew until then that avalanches made so much noise. They would roar down the hillsides and completely block the roads, probably causing the Germans more trouble than our actual demolitions!

We were still very vulnerable from the air and one day a German fighter patrol came over while we were fusing some of our mines and depth charges in a culvert on a road about halfway up the Romsdal Gorge. We were in an exposed position and could do little about taking effective cover. We just kept still, hoping the pilots would think we were a couple of sacks dropped off a passing lorry.

The fighters veered off and we breathed again, but too soon. We had not fooled them and I presume they made a quick radio check to see if any Germans should have been at that spot. Anyway, we suddenly heard the drone of aero engines again, rapidly getting louder, and the sergeant yelled: 'They're coming right at us, sir. Christ, they're low.'

At that moment we heard the rapid stutter of machine-guns, and I remember putting my arms round my head in an automatic gesture of protection. Useless as it was, it seemed to make me feel safer. In a moment or two the German fighters had zoomed over our heads and the ear-shattering clatter of guns stopped. The bullets had spattered harmlessly on the road above our heads and in fact they would have been lucky to hit us; two men curled up on the ground present a small and extremely difficult target for the guns in the wings of a diving plane.

I was furious at being the helpless victim of attack, unable to strike back. As I cursed out loud at the German race in general and these pilots in particular I suddenly had an idea. It seemed crazy, but it was better than doing nothing. I grabbed the sergeant by the arm. 'We'll try and bring one down with a depth charge.'

He was a wonderful chap, just the sort of companion for this type of operation. He obeyed orders first and asked questions afterwards, if there were any questions left by then. And he knew without my telling him that the fighters were circling round ready to dive at us again. I had noted their line of approach and it brought them more or less directly over one of our depth charges; this had given me the idea.

Quickly we fused the charge and I sent the sergeant away to shelter below the level of the road. Then, as I heard the German planes beginning their dive, I lit the fuse and raced for cover myself. Just as I flung myself down I heard the stutter of machine-guns again and almost at once the depth charge went off with a heavy crrrump. The machine-guns stopped abruptly and for one wonderful moment I thought we had got one of the fighters. But then I heard his engine as he throttled up to climb away and I could see as I lifted my head that he was undamaged. However, the Germans flew off and did not return.

We were pretty pleased with ourselves. We had hit back and frightened them off and it really had been too much to expect that we could bring a plane down. I have often wondered since what that particular pilot would have said if he had known what had gone off under his tail that day in Norway. He probably thought one of his bullets had hit a mine we had laid under the road and set it off. In fact he was almost certainly the first and only fighter pilot ever to be attacked from the ground by an anti-submarine depth charge!

We were now concentrating solely on finishing the job, surviving if we possibly could and getting back to Andalsnes. There were only three hours of darkness, which cut down our sleeping time but meant that we could get on with the demolitions faster. In another day or two we had just about finished, which was just as well, for our meagre food supplies had all but run out and we had barely enough fuel left to reach Andalsnes on the motor-bike.

With the working party we had left a couple of depth charges by a bridge that spanned a mountain stream running down from a glacier. I decided to make that our last fling. Unfortunately when I examined the bridge again I realized that the only effective demolition method was to get into the icy water and fix the charges to the piles that held it up.

It was one of the most unpleasant jobs I have ever tackled. Since our brush with the German fighters I had handled most of the demolition work myself, leaving the sergeant on watch, on his motor-bike. The fighters were still active and there was always the chance of an advance German patrol finding us. So I had no help fixing up the depth charges and the freezing blue water made me clumsy and slow. In all, I spent three hours in the grip of a cold clamminess that chilled me through until every part of my body was all but numb.

When the job was finished the sergeant had to haul my frozen, soaking carcass out of the water, carry it to the motorbike and drape it on the pillion seat. Back at the bungalow the stove was still going, thank God, and slowly I de-frosted and came alive again, a grim and painful process. To add to the discomfort we were both desperately hungry; by this time all our food had gone. We were down to the 'loot' we had found in the bungalow, which amounted to a bottle of raspberry wine and some curds and whey, all of which we polished off!

At the first sign of dawn we set out for Andalsnes. It occurred to me that the B.E.F. evacuation would be nearly over and that we would be among the last to go. I could hardly believe that I had been in Norway only a fortnight. Working in the snow with frozen fingers and racing along icy roads on the pillion of a motor-cycle seemed to have been my whole life and it was difficult just then to recall any other existence.

The sergeant was pushing the motor-bike along very gently now, coasting downhill, and he did a very expert job; we finally ran out of fuel at the crest of the hill which leads down into the town. As we free-wheeled along towards the harbour I noticed that the place looked pretty deserted. In the streets a few disconsolate-looking Norwegians were going about their business in the listless way that people have when they are waiting for a catastrophe which they know is on the way and which they can do nothing to stop. For the people of Andalsnes the catastrophe was German occupation.

I waved to several of them as we went by and they looked at us as if they could hardly believe their eyes. One or two shouted but I could not understand what they said. I assumed they were greeting us on our return, for our beards and general tatty appearance made it plain we had been away from civilization for a while. I shouted something meaningless back and waved again.

By the time we neared the harbour I was beginning to wonder what was going on. So far I had not seen a single British soldier, which was odd to say the least, and the harbour seemed very quiet; just a few Norwegian fishing boats at the quayside and not a sign of the hustle and bustle of evacuation.

The bike stopped at last and we dismounted and looked around. The peaceful harbour scene was much too peaceful for my liking.

'Are you thinking what I'm thinking, sir?' the sergeant asked.

'Probably, but let's find out for sure,' I replied, and went over to speak to a Norwegian fisherman. Eventually, from the few words of English he knew and the few words of Norwegian I knew, plus plenty of sign language, I confirmed the worst. All the British had gone. Presumably they had given us up for lost.

I explained that our only concern was to get out of Andalsnes somehow or other before the Germans got there, and that their advance patrols might be arriving at any time. Our Norwegian friend said he would see what he could do and went off to talk to some of his harbour colleagues. When he came back and told us his news my faith was restored in the luck of the Calverts, which I thought had deserted me at last. The news was that some relation of King Haakon had been left behind when the Royal Navy had evacuated the Norwegian royal family to Scotland, and a British warship was at that moment on its way up the fiord to pick him up and look for stragglers at the same time.

Sure enough a destroyer came into view soon afterwards and we waved frantically from the quayside like a couple of kids on Southend Pier; I had never been so glad to see a ship in all my life. The destroyer skipper paused only long enough to check our papers, then we were off again and bound for home.

Many of the weary and disillusioned troops who returned from the abortive landing in Norway were saying that B.E.F. stood for 'back every fortnight'; defeat, even an honourable one against overwhelming opposition, leaves a bitter taste in the mouth. But for me, though I wished we had had more success, that fortnight in Norway had been worth while. Apart from anything else, I believed I had established once and for all that I was better suited to the active life than to the world of desks and paper. Happily the powers-that-be agreed with me.

6

The British Guerrillas

Back home in England, Dunkirk was over and invasion fever was rapidly spreading. The Channel suddenly seemed very narrow, certainly not wide enough to keep the victorious German Army away from our shores for very long. After the disasters in France and the Low Countries our forces had little left to fight with except their courage and their bare hands, and these alone were not enough.

The men at the top had no advance knowledge of the strange decisions being made by Hitler's twisted brain. Poised on the coast of France his next step seemed all too obvious, and many months were to pass before it became clear that he had lost his opportunity of invading us. In the meantime we had to prepare as best we could to defend ourselves.

It was in this atmosphere of grim determination that a group of enlightened officers, who for some time had been putting forward Guerrilla-Commando-Special Force ideas without much success, began at last to find a hearing. Even then, in what Churchill called our darkest hour, it was necessary to think of attack as well as defence. Clearly we would be unable to launch any large-scale offensive for some considerable time ahead. But small raids by compact groups of highly trained men, aimed at selected targets where the impact would be far greater than could normally be achieved with a limited force, were still possible. A number of quick stabs at vital spots would keep the enemy under pressure, boost the morale of occupied countries and also keep the peckers up at home. The cost would be comparatively small, well worth while for the results obtained.

So the arguments went, and eventually they were accepted. A Special Training Centre was set up at Lochailort in Scotland under Colonel Coates, late C.O. of the 5th Scots Guards; Lord Lovat, who later became a famous Commando leader, was chief instructor. Bill and David Stirling, who had been among the volunteers for Finland in the 'Phoney Fifth' and went on to do great things in the Special Air Service, were also there. And I was sent up, fresh from my Norwegian adventures, as instructor in demolitions.

It was good to be in the company of men who were pioneering the type of fighting that had begun to intrigue me: the small force which acted on its own, harried the enemy and upset their balance. Such forces could not win wars alone, of course, and none of us ever pretended that they could. But they had tremendous value as the spearhead of a big attack, or the annoying jolt which distracted the enemy from the central front, or the means of destroying a vital strategic point which for some reason or other the main force could not reach. They could dart in quickly and silently from the air, from the sea or on land and do their deadly work before the other side really knew what was going on.

Another form in which a Special Force could be a great asset to any commander, as we showed later in Burma, was as a harrying group actually operating behind enemy lines. On any battlefront, particularly where communications and supplies are at full stretch for maybe hundreds of miles, there is a high concentration of troops in the immediate forward area, backed by reserve, supply, service and headquarters units. But these thin out rapidly behind the front, leaving a gap where a small force can work with telling effect on roads and railways, disrupting supplies and generally creating mayhem. This was the role of the Chindits in Burma, and jungle country was particularly suited to this type of operation. But the success of large bands of Resistance fighters in occupied countries during the war showed that it was equally possible in many parts of the Western Hemisphere.

After six stimulating weeks at Lochailort I was suddenly called back to the War Office. I was annoyed at being dragged away from my friends in Scotland but I felt a little better about it when I was told to report to one of the lesser-known sections of the Military Intelligence Directorate. Evidently this was something special.

As so often happened when one was recalled for an 'urgent' job, I had to hang around waiting. At the War Office I passed the time by writing a paper called 'The operations of small forces behind the enemy lines supplied and supported by air'. In this I tried to put down my ideas in detail, backed by what I had learned in Norway and up at Lochailort. By this time I was quite convinced that troops could live for weeks or even months entirely on air drops, which could provide ammunition and reinforcements as well as food and clothing. This meant that a Special Force could operate in any type of terrain with tremendous manoeuvrability; working behind enemy lines, here one minute and gone the next, they could be a real headache to any army.

However, I had to put away my thoughts on this subject for the next few months. The job for which I had been brought from Scotland was concerned with defence and was centred in Kent and Sussex, the main invasion danger areas of England at that time. I was told I would be working with another officer, who turned out to be Peter Fleming[1], the author and traveller. When we met at the War Office I was still a temporary captain with a substantive Regular rank of subaltern; Peter was a full captain but a part-time soldier from the Reserve. This was the sort of situation that often cropped up during the war and sometimes led to difficult situations. Peter and I, however, became good friends and worked well together in the unusual tasks we were ordered to carry out.

Briefly, our job was to make Kent and Sussex as unsafe and unpleasant as possible for the Germans if they ever got that far. Our instructions came as something of a shock to me. I had been caught up, along with everyone else, by the invasion fever, but this official recognition that desperate measures might soon be needed brought home, as nothing else had, the full gravity of our situation in 1940. We had treated the invasion scare half as a joke, as the British are inclined to do; but clearly the dreaded danger of occupation was all too real.

Peter and I started by trying to put ourselves in the place of invaders, seeing the towns and villages of Kent and Sussex for the first time and not admiring the scenery but deciding which bridges to cross, which houses to occupy and so on. We then set about mining and booby-trapping all the places we thought the Germans would use.

We covered bridges and railway lines first, then sorted out the big houses which would have made good headquarters and billets. Most of them had cellars or basements of some kind and we crammed them

---

[1] Brother of the famous writer Ian Fleming, creator of James Bond, 007. Peter was a famous writer and traveller himself.

full of explosives which would be quite safe until a secret switch was pressed to start up a time fuse.

The next job was to pick the right people who could be relied upon to find their way to a switch and press it when the Germans had taken over. Mostly we chose farmers or farm workers, solid chaps who were not likely to lose their heads under the sort of pressures that occupation brings. But there were other people as well, quite ordinary types in normal, everyday jobs, who were entrusted with our secrets and would, I am sure, have given the Germans a most uncomfortable time if they had ever landed in England. There were even one or two country parsons among them!

Nearly all these brave and willing people had brothers, sons or nephews in the forces and the knowledge that they, too, had been asked to 'do their bit' seemed to give them a quiet satisfaction. Quiet it had to be, for they could tell no one else about it. These were the people who would have formed the nucleus of a resistance movement in Britain. None of them knew who the others were but they would have got together somehow. And they would not have stopped at one blow against the hated invader any more than the French or the Dutch or the Norwegians did.

With this in mind we laid in stores for them at well-hidden points. There were food and water, clothing, medical supplies and explosives. I also prepared ready-made booby traps for them to use, such as innocent-looking milk chums filled with the explosive ammonal. The farmers among our volunteers would have had no difficulty in placing these where they would do most damage.

I remember one leathery-faced old character who worked on a farm on the Romney Marsh. He had fought in France in World War I and his two sons were now in the Navy. 'Don't you worry,' he told me. 'If any of them Huns try to settle in around here they'll soon wish they was somewhere else.' He said it simply and directly; he almost seemed to be looking forward to the prospect. It was a comforting thought at the time, when invasion seemed so near, that we were preparing the ground for a resistance movement to carry on the fight if we should fail to keep back the enemy.

Another of our assignments was to cast the same, invader-like eye along the south-eastern coastline. Beaches were already being mined and covered in barbed wire and pillboxes. But it was clearly time to do something about the piers at the resorts. They were no longer pleasant amusements for holiday makers but inviting landing places for the Germans. There was no room for sentiment. The piers were clearly a danger to the country as they stood and it was decided they would have to be dealt with.

I was concerned with the piers at Brighton, Worthing and Eastbourne – where I had often enjoyed myself while at prep school. First we blew up the centre sections, leaving two parts standing. These, we hoped, would prove tempting to the invaders and we planned a welcome with booby traps. Fun-fairs became filled with potential death. Penny-in-the-slot machines would blow up at a touch. No German would see what the butler saw. And if a jack-booted soldier carefully avoided the machines he would be caught by the trip wires which crisscrossed the broad-walk.

It was while we were working on Brighton Pier that I learned a valuable lesson. We were feeling very pleased with ourselves as we laid every type of trap we could think of and covered up our fancy work to persuade the enemy that every thing was as innocent as it looked. Suddenly a seagull swooped down, touched one of the trip wires and set off a trap.

We nearly jumped out of our skins at the unexpected explosion. 'What the bloody hell was that,' yelled a Sapper sergeant working near me. Then he spotted the seagull, which had wheeled smartly away in the split-second before the bang and was completely unharmed. 'I bet that bird's a Jerry bastard,' the sergeant growled and we all began to laugh.

But we didn't laugh for long. A piece of pier planking blown up by the first explosion landed on another of our carefully laid traps and set it off, the debris from that fired another and so on. They went on playing leap-frog with each other as we backed down the pier before them and prepared to jump into the sea.

Fortunately the explosions stopped as suddenly as they had started and we did not get the ducking that we probably deserved for not appreciating the folly of laying booby traps too close to one another. Now we knew that by putting them further apart we could avoid the risk of one chance explosion ruining the lot. We acted on it then and the lesson proved very useful to me later in Burma and Malaya.

Several years after the war ended I met an ex-mayor of Brighton.

When he heard who I was he remembered the part I played in wrecking the pier there and made it clear in forceful style that he was still very angry. Apparently it had cost the town a lot of money to get the pier ready for holidaymakers again after the war. I have sometimes wondered what he would have said if the pier had been left as it was and the Germans had used it to land in Brighton back in 1940.

Apart from our work in creating defences against the Germans, we were also given the job of testing out some of the defences set up by other people. At that time the troops standing by in Kent and Sussex to repel invaders were under the command of a promising young general named Montgomery. The qualities that later made him one of the great commanders of the war were already apparent to those who worked with him. Alertness had always been his watchword and Peter and I knew we had a job on our hands when we were told to test the security of his headquarters in a big country house in Kent.

There was no secret about our job. Monty's security police knew all about us and what we had been told to do. We therefore decided on a double bluff.

All the pubs in the area were checked as a matter of course by the security police so we visited them in turn, talking loudly to anyone who would listen about our plan to make a frontal attack on Monty's H.Q.

'There's a terrace with flower pots along it,' we would say after sinking a pint or two. 'We're just going to stroll up and plant a stick of gelignite in each one.'

Everyone in the bar would roar with laughter and some of the civilians probably wondered privately how on earth two loud-mouthed idiots like us had ever got commissions in the Army. Monty's police, of course, credited us with a little more intelligence. Obviously this story we were blurting about was just a cover-up for something entirely different. Having seen through our rather obvious ruse they joined in the laughter, ordered another beer and spent the rest of the evening trying to work out what our real plan would be.

On a dark, moonless night soon afterwards Peter and I approached Monty's H.Q. across the fields and slipped past the sentries with little trouble. They had presumably been warned to keep a special look-out, but after our antics in the pubs the security men probably thought we would come in disguised as the laundry or something equally clever. Anyway, there were no special precautions that we could see.

Using all the cover available in the darkness we crawled around the edge of the lawn and put our explosives, with time fuses attached, into the flower pots, just as we had said we would. It was all too easy and the success rather went to our heads. While I stayed outside on watch Peter actually went into the house, where he found the officer of the day asleep in the ground-floor duty room. Feeling this was too good a chance to miss, Peter tied a booby trap to the officer's leg. it would make a loud but harmless bang and perhaps slightly singe the chap's leg; nothing more. Peter then rejoined me and we got away without being spotted.

The next morning we reported to Monty at the house. He was in a jovial mood. 'Well, you couldn't make it then, eh?' he said. 'Not as good as you thought, are you? Couldn't beat our defences here.'

I told him that we had completed our mission. 'We approached the house unmolested and "wiped it out" with high explosives as instructed, sir.'

Monty looked astonished. 'Look here, Calvert,' he said, 'I think you're making it all up. My chaps got your measure. I don't believe you were here at all.'

Peter looked at me and we both looked at our watches. It was about time for our bangers to work but time fuses are not always reliable. Suddenly there was an explosion outside on the terrace. Monty swung round, looking quite pale. 'Turn out the guard! See what that is,' he shouted.

There was another bang and then the flower pots went up one by one. We had put something small in them, just enough to make a bang and break them up. But it was quite noisy in the room for a moment or two.

After the first shock Monty took it in very good part. He laughed and said: 'Well, gentlemen, obviously you have been here before. I apologize. Have a drink.'

It occurred to me that he would not be so hospitable to the officer in charge of security when he had a word with him after we had gone. As for the sleeping officer of the day, we had not mentioned him and Monty hadn't either. Presumably the chap had kept quiet, which was good judgement on his part.

There was no country-house atmosphere about the headquarters Peter and I had adopted. We operated from an old barn where our stand-ins for furniture were boxes of gelignite, which is perfectly safe as long as it is treated the right way. On one occasion we had a visit from several V.I.P.s and decided we would have to do the right thing and offer them a meal. It was quite nourishing, though not West End standard, and we all sat down round the box of gelignite that we were using as a table.

Soon after we had started it began to get dark so I lit a few candles and put them on the box. This was normal practice for Peter and me and we went on eating without giving a second thought to the spluttering candle flames. Looking back I realize that our guests, not used to living on quite such intimate terms with high explosives, behaved very well in the circumstances.

'I see you like to live dangerously,' was the dry comment made between mouthfuls by General Sir Andrew Thorne, commander of XII Corps (Kent and Sussex).

Whatever danger Peter and I may have been in at that time it was certainly nothing compared with the perils facing the pilots who were fighting out the Battle of Britain over our heads as we worked. When the R.A.F. won their decisive victory and convinced Hitler that the Luftwaffe could never gain air superiority over Britain, they also swept away any remaining fears of immediate invasion.

Peter and I were recalled. And I remember thinking as we returned to London that, if it had been called to action, the Resistance Army of Kent and Sussex would have had at its core some of the toughest and most determined men I had ever met. Their farms and their shops and their homes would have been highly dangerous places for any enemy soldier to enter. Although the Germans didn't know it, they should have thanked the R.A.F. boys for keeping them away from Britain.

7

Back to the East

Up at Lochailort the commando school was flourishing and it was decided to send a mission to Australia in October, 1940, to set up a similar school out there. I was selected as one of the instructors, which meant that two years after my return from Shanghai I was on my way East again.

Before I went I was told to find a weapons training instructor to take with me; I could have anyone I wanted and no commanding officer would be allowed to stop the posting. Time was short and I went down to the Small Arms School at Hythe, in Kent, which I thought would be as good a place as any to find the right chap.

My mind was buzzing with a dozen thoughts on the trip down: how good it was to be on my way to Australia, a country I had always wanted to see; what it would be like trying to teach the tough Aussies to be even tougher; what the chances were of the Japs starting something in the Pacific and how I would be right on the spot as soon as they did. The immediate task in hand took up little time among these interesting cogitations; choosing an instructor for weapon training was just a necessary routine job. I had no way of knowing that I was about to meet a man who would be at my side in and out of fights and battles for some time to come, and who would remain a loyal, tried and trusted friend.

At Hythe I wandered round the school watching the instructors at work and soon spotted the sort of chap I was looking for. He was a sergeant of Cockney stock, tall, lean and obviously as tough as they come. His name was Peter Stafford and when I told him the job I had to offer he accepted without a moment's hesitation. This quick, straight-forward decision impressed me and it was then I had the first inkling that I had picked a winner.

From Australia Peter went on with me to Burma, got his commission and became my adjutant and eventually my second-in-command. And that first visit to Australia showed him a country after his own adventurous heart; he married an Australian girl and now lives at St. Kilda, near Melbourne.

Among the other instructors on the mission was Freddie Spencer Chapman,[1] the mountaineer and explorer. We became great friends and Freddie taught me fieldcraft and tracking, or as much of these two fascinating crafts as I could take in. They stood me in good stead later on in the jungle.

We set up our school at a wild place called Wilson's Promontory, on the southern tip of Australia where it points down towards Tasmania. It was miles from anywhere and an ideal spot for commando training because it gave us a wide choice of different types of country within a reasonable area: mountains, plains, forests, sand dunes and sea. Our job was to train Australian and New Zealand officers and N.C.O.s, who then went off to train their own men in commando methods, and to form what were known as the Independent Companies. We had a pretty tight schedule but I managed to learn a lot from Freddie in any free moments we could get.

When I feel like boasting I invariably bring out my old story which begins: 'You know, in all my time on active service I was never once ambushed . . .' I then go on to recall all the times when I could have been but wasn't because I spotted the trap before walking into it. In fact this is all perfectly true and the main reason, apart from the luck of the Calverts, was that I learned so much from Freddie.

The first big lesson he taught me was always to be on the look-out for the likely ambush spot, such as the piece of rising ground ahead covered with rocks or trees or high undergrowth. In the sort of warfare we were concerned with this had to be an automatic task as the eyes took in the surroundings at any given moment. It might be necessary to lay a sudden ambush to trap an enemy patrol and the spot where this was most likely to succeed was also a spot to approach with the utmost caution.

---

[1] Freddie Spencer Chapman was later a member of a 'stay-behind' force of volunteers who moved into the jungle when Malaya fell. The story of his three years surviving the Japs and the jungle can be read in his highly recommended book *The Jungle is Neutral*.

The second lesson which Freddie taught me, and which saved my life more than once, was that birds stopped singing, and most other wild animals also became quiet and still, when human beings were near them. The sudden silence in the jungle when the twitterings and squeaks and grunts that were hardly noticeable most of the time were abruptly turned off – that silence, first demonstrated to me on Wilson's Promontory by Freddie, has shouted out in Burma and Malaya and kept me out of endless trouble.

I also learned a great deal from the Australians and New Zealanders at the school, especially about explosives, which many of them had had great experience in using as gold miners. Altogether I was enjoying myself and during 1941 I became chief instructor and was promoted major. But once again, although I loved the open-air life and was probably fitter than I had ever been before, I was chafing, as I had done in London in 1939, at not being able to get mixed up in a real scrap somewhere. I even considered deserting, changing my name and joining the Australian Army in the hope of getting some action. But then I heard I was to be posted, to a job which had exciting possibilities.

I was being sent off to Burma to become chief instructor at the Bush Warfare School in Maymyo, the summer capital, where British and Australian officers and N.C.O.s were taught the rudiments of guerrilla fighting before going in to help the Chinese. This was before Pearl Harbour and the Japs were not yet in our war. In fact, one of the main aims of helping the Chinese to use guerrilla tactics was to enable them to tie up as many Jap troops as possible in China itself and keep Nipponese thoughts away from further conquests in the Pacific. The Americans had an air warfare mission in Burma with a similar aim.

All this made the Burma training job very interesting and, unless I was very much mistaken, it could lead to even more intriguing possibilities. It was pretty plain to most of us in the Far East that it was only a matter of time before the Japs started something outside China and that we could only hope to delay the inevitable, which was war between Japan and the Allies. When that came Burma would be in the thick of it and, with this posting, I would be in Burma. All in all I was convinced that before many more months had passed I would be crossing swords again with my old enemy of Shanghai days, the Japs.

What we were doing in Maymyo was, of course, very unneutral. The name Bush Warfare School was in itself a deception. We were not preparing people to fight in the Burma jungle; our task was to train officers and N.C.O.s to lead guerrillas in the plains of China, a very different type of warfare. But, in view of our on-the-surface impartiality in the Japanese-Chinese conflict, we could hardly give the mission its proper title, which would have been something like China Guerrilla Training School.

The school was split up for training purposes into cadres known as 'commandos', to confuse the situation even more. This deception was also part of the deliberate policy, but unfortunately it ultimately deceived many of our own people as well as the Japs. When the Jap war finally began the school was criticized – by General Alexander, among others, who took over as C.-in-C. Burma at the time of the retreat – for not having done its job of training commando troops to fight in the Burma jungle! As we had never set out to do this the criticisms made us extremely angry, but events were moving so rapidly that there was no time to explain the position and we just had to accept it philosophically. As far as Alex was concerned it was probably not his fault that he blamed us; almost certainly no one at H.Q. would have explained to him when he took over what the 'commandos' at the 'Bush Warfare School' really were. Therefore it was hardly surprising that he took the words at their face value. It was just another case of a headquarters mix-up for which the men in the field carried the can. Soon after arriving at the school I had been appointed commandant, so in this case I did most of the carrying.

Many years later, in 1958, volume two of the official series *The War Against Japan* was published, and backed up my version of the affair. It said that I had been 'in charge of the Bush Warfare School at Maymyo, training British guerrillas for use in China'. It has taken a long time to clear my name officially of that particular charge and by 1958 no one seemed to care very much anyway. However, it gave me a little private satisfaction.

The surprise Japanese raid on the American Fleet at Pearl Harbour came at the beginning of December, 1941, and Jap attacks started on Malaya almost at once. Before the end of December Japanese planes were bombing Rangoon, the capital of Burma, and in the middle of January, 1942, the Japanese Army began its rapid advance into Burma from Siam. Towards the end of

February it was clearly just a matter of days before Rangoon fell.[2]

By this time many of my instructors had gone off to fight, either in China itself with the men we had been training or with the Chinese troops in Burma who were also vainly trying to stem the Jap advance. I was still at the school in Maymyo with a hard core of about forty or fifty British and Australian officers, N.C.O.s and other ranks, Peter Stafford among them.

The swiftness of the Jap advance, backed by their superiority in numbers and equipment, had come as a shock to many people who had never seen the Japs fight and imagined that our troops, even with their poor and outdated equipment, were a match for 'any bunch of damned Orientals'. The shock of defeat, or impending defeat, generally leads to a certain amount of confusion and the situation at that time was fluid, to say the least.

I was getting pretty fed up myself at being left to keep the school ticking over while desperate battles were being fought against an enemy I really did know something about. Demanding a posting would be hopeless in that chaotic atmosphere; but I had to do something. So I thought up a plan of my own.

I knew from my friends at headquarters in Maymyo that an Australian Division on its way home from the Middle East was expected to be diverted in an attempt to hold back the Japanese advance through Burma. I also knew that there was some disagreement between British Prime Minister Winston Churchill and Australian Prime Minister John Curtin about whether this diversion should be carried out. It seemed probable that the Japs might have an inkling of what was going on and it occurred to me that I had the means to persuade them even further that the Australian reinforcements had in fact arrived. Some of my men at the school were Aussies and we all had Australian bush hats, which I had taken along with me when I went to Maymyo. (This type of hat, incidentally, was later adopted by the whole of the Army in Burma.) My plan was to carry out a piece of deception by leading a party of my men, all wearing bush hats, in raids against the advancing Japanese. With any luck we could convince them that we were the

---

[2] On 8th March, Rangoon fell. General Alexander and his staff were nearly captured on their way out.

Australian reinforcements and make them take counter-moves which would slow them up.

In some ways, although we all like to win, a retreat has its advantages. In an attack the moves are carefully planned and everything is nice and orderly; in a retreat the whole place is in chaos and the situation is more open to individual initiative if one is that way inclined. So, having decided on my plan, I set off with my chaps down to Prome, a town on the Irrawaddy about 150 miles north of Rangoon and now the hastily organized headquarters of our 17th Division.

The whole place was in pretty much of a shambles. Rangoon had just fallen and it was anyone's guess how much longer we could hang on in Burma. Units had been broken up and mixed up and altogether there was a rather desperate air about the place. I reported to a senior staff officer who was tired, depressed and harassed and looked as if he hadn't had time to wash or sleep for a week.

'I have about seventy men, sir,' I reported, after a few short preliminaries.

He waved a weary hand. 'Look after the west bank of the Irrawaddy,' he said. 'We're very exposed there.'

That was good enough for me. A vague order, nothing detailed, was just what I wanted. It gave me elbow room to put my deception into effect and for the time being I became a temporary Australian! All my men, needless to say, were only too pleased at the prospect of some action and I was also lucky enough to meet a Marine officer, Major Johnstone, who volunteered to bring his men along. There were about a dozen Marines altogether and they had their own launch on the Irrawaddy. The operation they were supposed to have been in had been put off and they were hanging about in the general confusion at Prome with nothing to do. I was very pleased to have them with me and they fought like tigers when the time came.

8

Showboat Raid

It must have been one of the strangest raids of the war. With my scratch company of volunteers I set off behind the Japanese lines aboard a curious, two-storeyed river craft that would have been more at home as a Mississippi showboat than an Irrawaddy troop carrier. And alongside, like a duckling following its mother, came the Marines' launch.

None of the staff people had time to bother their heads about a show like ours so I had been left to do my own organizing, such as arranging for ammunition, demolition explosives, food, water and so on. None of this was difficult in Prome at that time as long as one knew the right people to approach. The main difficulty, however, was transport, particularly getting hold of something big enough to take us all. I had almost begun to despair when I came across this weird-looking double-decker. It had originally been a passenger boat of the Irrawaddy Flotilla Company plying between Rangoon and Myitkyina, a long trip which called for a sizeable craft.

Odd as it looked, the old showboat went along well enough and had already been helping out with the evacuation. The crew were Burmese but their skipper was an Englishman called Rea, who was an old Irrawaddy Flotilla sailor and was only too willing to come along with us. He was an ex-navy man who had served on minesweepers in the First World War and had only one kidney. On this trip he proved to be worth his weight in gold.

After we had scrounged as much ammunition, explosive, food and drink as we could we set off in good spirits, flying the Union Jack. We certainly stood no chance of stopping the Jap advance by striking some daring blow at their vitals; this type of thing is reserved for the heroes of movieland. At best we would be able to annoy the Japs by

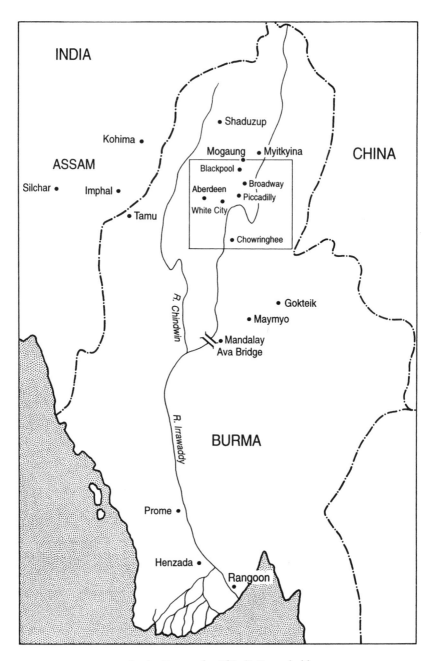

In the Rectangle: Chindit Strongholds

demolitions and a few raids here and there, generally upsetting them. All this would be bad for their morale, which must have been pretty good at that moment and was certainly ripe for a knock or two. General Slim was planning a counter-attack, as soon as the 1st Burma Division could link up with him. We could keep the Japs happy on the west bank of the Irrawaddy whilst he concentrated his forces. Slim and the 17th Division were still offensive-minded.

Looking back on that river trip it amazes me that any of us survived. One well-placed shell could have knocked us out of the water. But, as I had thought back in Maymyo, the Japs were thin on the ground along the river banks. Their mobile artillery was following up close behind the main advance and used the roads, or what passed for roads, to make better speed. There had been no time to post guns, or even adequate infantry forces, along the river and the Japs were obviously thinking this of secondary importance to a swift advance.

The river itself was half a mile wide in some places but difficult to navigate at times because of extensive mud banks. Captain Rea did a wonderful job keeping us out of the mud. We would have been in real trouble if the old showboat had stuck for good; on land our chances of getting back would have been considerably restricted. As it was we made steady progress and stopped off whenever we saw a likely target for our explosives. We blasted several holes in the railway, blew up trucks, wrecked bridges and sank any boat or barge that looked big enough to be of use to the Japs.

The general drill whenever we went ashore was to put down lay-back positions to give covering fire in case the demolition parties were attacked and had to beat a hasty retreat. We had one or two clashes with small Jap patrols but they did not seem very bothered about us. Presumably their orders were to press on with the main advance and leave stragglers or any odd pockets of resistance to be mopped up later. This would have been a normal procedure for swiftly moving troops and it did not occur to them at the time that we were deliberately penetrating behind their lines.

Most of the places we stopped at were jungle villages of varying sizes, the populations of which had reached a state of resignation that Oriental people can achieve so much more readily than the European races. They did nothing to hinder our landings or our demolition work and it was quite clear that the majority, at least, would do nothing to oppose the Japs either. At these villages I would also send a few of my Australians ashore to act a little tipsy and boast about the strength of their newly arrived brigade. This talk, I knew, would soon reach the Japs via the local informers. At selected places I left a few Aussies behind with orders to show themselves occasionally and to keep on the move along the banks, partly to create the impression of greater numbers and partly to avoid the risk of attack by a Jap patrol.

By the time we reached the town of Henzada I was feeling fairly satisfied that we had caused some useful havoc and achieved most of what we had set out to do. It was now nearly time we turned back, but Henzada was by far the biggest place we had come to, about the size of Eastbourne, and I decided to look round there first. The river was low at the time and we tied up behind flood banks about forty feet high. The banks were there for protection during the monsoon and would give us excellent cover from the shore in case of trouble. I ordered most of the chaps to land and put down strong lay-back positions on low-lying ground between the river and the town and also on the reverse side of the flood banks. Then I set off with a small party to see what we could find.

Our entry into the main part of the town caused quite a lot of interest and we exchanged friendly waves and shouted greetings with some of the people, who appeared to be more alert and intelligent than the villagers along the river. By the time we reached what was obviously some sort of main square we had collected quite a following.

I decided this was a perfect opportunity to further my deception about the Australian reinforcements and indicated, through an interpreter we had brought along from the boat, that I would like to say a few words to the assembled company. The idea appealed to the Burmese and we were led to the top of a broad flight of steps leading into a large public building facing on to the square.

It was the first time I had attempted a speech before quite such a large public and I began to feel nervous as I looked out at the expectant brown faces gazing at me. It was a very hot day and the sweat poured down my forehead and into my eyes as I wondered what to say. I began to wish like hell I was somewhere else. Then I pulled myself together and began telling the crowd that we were the advance party of a big army of Australians who were coming to chase the Japanese out of Burma. As the Burmese interpreter from Captain

Rea's crew translated my words there was a buzz of excitement in the square. This encouraged me to go on and explain how we intended to throw out the hated invader and restore peace to the land, and so on. Everyone in the crowd seemed to be hanging on my words and I was beginning to enjoy myself. But not for long.

Suddenly, at the back of the square, men in uniform leaped to their feet and a voice shouted in English: 'Lay down your arms. You are surrounded.' We had been surprised by a group of the Burmese 'traitor' army led by Japanese officers. And for a moment, caught in mid-speech, I was completely taken aback.

But one of the men on the steps with me, a corporal named Maddox, stepped in and gave the Japs the only possible answer: 'Balls!' His cry echoed round the square and at that instant he let fly with his tommy-gun. The crowd in the square fell flat on their faces as we all fired rapid bursts at the enemy. We then leapt off the steps and beat a hasty retreat back towards the Irrawaddy.

We had a good start on the Japs who, not knowing our showboat was waiting, must have thought they would trap us by the river. They were in for a shock. The chaps I had left behind kept themselves well under cover and they had a good view of our pursuers as we panted past; I almost felt sorry for those Japs as they ran straight into the bullets from our positions. By the time they retreated numbers of them were dead and a number of others wounded. Our casualties were two men slightly wounded.

It was more than likely that the Japs would have reinforcements close at hand. They were the largest enemy group we had come across so far, bigger than a normal patrol, and they might even have mobile artillery in support. Obviously, the quicker we got on the move the better. I ordered a swift withdrawal on to the showboat while the Japs were licking their wounds. We were already on the move when I was told that a few of our men were still ashore. They had been at a point furthest from the boat and the withdrawal order had not reached them. By the time they realized what was happening and began to move towards us the Japs had re-formed and were advancing on the river.

I was determined not to leave anyone behind; I ordered the boat back, then called to half a dozen men to come ashore with me. But the Japs had us in their sights now and we could not get past the flood banks, which they were strafing with machine-guns. So I put as many men as possible on to the metal roof of the showboat to give us covering fire while we had another go at getting ashore.

The battle was hotting up and the Japs had brought up mortars. Luckily their range was rather short and the shells landed on the banks, showering us with mud but nothing worse. Our covering fire proved effective; we made a quick dash ashore and managed to scramble the other chaps on board. The Marines did a particularly fine job in drawing fire away from us and keeping the Jap machine-gunners pinned down.

Peter Stafford was by my side and we were the last two to go aboard after a quick look round to make sure no one else had been left behind. I remember how idiotically polite we were as the mortar shells fell around us.

'Up you go, Peter,' I said.

'No, after you, sir.'

'Don't arse about, man, get aboard.'

I could see he was still prepared to argue but at that moment a shell fell really close, covering us in mud, and we hauled ourselves aboard feeling slightly foolish.

Captain Rea was all set and had the old showboat on the move as soon as we hit the deck. But our troubles were not over yet. Rea had to turn the boat round before we could get under way and we were in full view of the Japs while he carried out this tricky manoeuvre. Earlier on we had run aground and been forced to dump all our sandbags overboard to give us more buoyancy to get afloat again. So I had ordered all our rations to be stacked round the top deck to replace the sandbags as cover. We flung ourselves down behind the tins and packets and bags and joined the covering party in keeping up a steady stream of fire on shore until we were finally out of range.

When we were able to sit back and look around us Peter picked up a tin of sausages in front of him and showed it to me. There were a number of dents and holes in it where bullets had hit the tin and ricocheted off the rounded surface. He reckoned the sausages saved his life and as far as I know still has that tin at his home in Australia.

Four of our chaps had been killed and seven wounded in the battle at Henzada, a surprisingly small casualty list considering all the lead that had been flying about. But we were now seventy miles from Prome and I decided we had better start on our way back. Also, I didn't want to leave the small groups of Australians alone for too long along the river banks.

I reported our action to Prome by wireless and was then told to report back in person as soon as possible in the Marines' launch; another officer would be sent down river to take over from me. I was unhappy about this for it meant I had to hand over a bluff, one that I had conceived myself and more or less played by ear as I went along. It would be very difficult for another man to take charge successfully, whoever he was; but my orders were clear enough and I had no choice but to obey. Unfortunately, some time after I left, the situation along the Irrawaddy deteriorated and the showboat party was attacked by the Japs, suffering about fifty per cent casualties.

Meanwhile, back at Prome, I had expected to be congratulated on a successful raid. But I should have known better. Instead of congratulations I received a sharp rebuke for endangering the lives of civilians of the Irrawaddy Flotilla Company and damaging property of the Burmah Oil Company during my demolition operations. The fact that this would fall into the hands of the Japanese anyway was ignored.

Again it was many years before my actions were justified publicly. In his memoirs Field Marshal Viscount Slim wrote of the poor state of affairs when he took over Burma Corps early in 1942. He went on to speak of my 'daring raid by river on Henzada', and another surprise raid by the 1st Gloucesters, and added: 'There was obviously a great deal of fight in the 17th Division.' To Slim, at least, our show of thrust and attack, amid so much retreat and defeat, had been worth while. I also learned later that my main object had been achieved and that for a while the Japanese believed an Australian brigade had landed in Burma and changed their plans accordingly.

At the time, however, I felt pretty fed up with the treatment I had received. I made my way back to Maymyo and decided that what I needed was a few drinks and a day or two's rest. So I was not at all pleased when I reached the Bush Warfare School and heard that a senior officer was paying a visit.

I stamped into my office and found that my visitor, a brigadier, was in fact sitting at my desk. Normally this would not have bothered me particularly but in my present weary and disgruntled mood it got under my skin. I was in command here and this was my office and whoever the stranger was, he was not entitled to sit in *that* chair.

I glared at him and said: 'Who are you?'

He was quite calm and composed. 'Wingate,' he replied.

The name meant nothing to me but this did not worry him. 'Who are you?' he asked, in return.

I was pretty filthy after the trip and it was a fair question. 'Calvert,' I said, and added: 'Excuse me, but that's my desk.'

'I'm sorry.' He moved aside at once and let me sit down.

In spite of my unpleasant mood I was impressed. He showed no resentment at this somewhat disrespectful treatment by a major. He began talking quietly, asking questions about the showboat raid. And to my surprise they were the right sort of questions.

Tired as I was I soon began to realize that this was a man I could work for and follow. Clearly he knew all that I knew about unconventional warfare and a lot more; he was streets ahead of anyone else I had spoken to, including the Lochailort boys. Suddenly I no longer felt tired. For even at that first meeting something of the driving inspiration inside Orde Wingate transferred itself to me.

9

Wingate

Much has already been written about Wingate. He has been attacked and defended, blamed for wrong decisions and praised for right ones, accused of being a butcher, a showman and many other things and in turn exonerated on all these charges. I have no wish to start up any further controversy over the bones of a brave man who was once my leader and my friend. But this is my story and Wingate is a part of it, a very vital part. And unfortunately he was – and still is, even in his grave – the sort of man the very mention of whose name sparks off controversy, like striking a flint under a petrol-sodden rag.

I am no military historian and it is not my object here to analyse a battle or an operation or a phase of the war and point out the brilliant manoeuvres that were carried out or the strategic or tactical errors that were made. Enough of that has been done already – too often by people who were far from the scene of events. My analysis is simply that we fought like hell in Burma and, in the end, we won. My belief is that Wingate paved the way for our victory because he was not only a bold general but also an inspiring leader.

As I said at the beginning of this book, he was an unconventional soldier and an unconventional man, and therefore so much of what he did and what he stood for created enmity and bitterness in those around him. That, I suppose, is a cross that the rebellious ones have to bear in any walk of life. I like to think that in the time I was associated with Orde Wingate I helped him to carry this cross, though in fact he was quite capable of doing so unaided.

Soon after we met I began to realize he was an outstanding soldier and did not try to disguise to others what I felt, though often it was not a popular view. In the years since his death, with plenty of time to think back upon what he achieved, I have become more than ever convinced that I was right. Peter Fleming has written elsewhere that I was 'unquestionably thought of by Wingate as the heir to his doctrine and tradition'. Many people will say that, although I was not chosen to succeed him when the time came, my opinion of Wingate is hopelessly biased because it was to him that I owed my swift promotion. My reply, in advance, is that I freely admit bias; not, however, because of blind loyalty but because I came to know Wingate better than most and had the opportunity to see and to study him in all his various moods.

It was strange that I had never heard of him before we met that day in February, 1942, at my office in Maymyo. For he had been extremely active in guerrilla fighting methods for several years before the outbreak of the Second World War, and I thought I knew nearly everyone in the Army who was interested in this line.

Wingate, however, had not been half-playing at it as I had been in Hong Kong and Norway. I had had to feel my way, improvising and 'playing by ear'. Again, at Lochailort, which came after Norway, the whole business of commando and special force warfare had seemed new and exciting to those of us who thought we were in at the beginning. How wrong we were! Wingate, by this time, was an old hand who had tried out in action most of our 'new' theories, discarded or improved them, thought up further original methods and put them into execution against enemy forces. Which is why he was able to ask the right questions about my Irrawaddy raid and put his finger unerringly on the lessons to be learned from it. He was, as I have said, streets ahead of the rest of us.

From 1928 until 1933 Wingate had served with the Sudan Defence Force and it was during this period that he became fluent in Arabic and gained his profound knowledge of the Middle East. Because of this he was sent for when bands of Arab rebels and outlaws were on the rampage in Palestine and Transjordan in 1936, causing, among other things, quite a lot of damage to oil installations in the desert.

Wingate raised, trained and led a force of Jewish volunteers and by 1938 order had been restored. The crafty Arabs had been outwitted on their own territory by Wingate's guerrilla tactics and he was awarded the D.S.O. His success had another important sequel: Wingate had shown the Jews that they could fight and beat the Arabs; this was something they had forgotten for 2,000 years but, thanks to Wingate, they did not forget in 1948, when they routed the Egyptians. Undoubtedly the Jews thought very highly of Wingate's leadership and I think it is true that had he lived he would have been offered command of the Israeli Army.

There was, unfortunately, another side to all this. Many of the people who thought that they would harm him in the Army declared that Wingate himself was a Jew, which was not true. He treated these attempts to damage his career with contempt and often added fuel to the fire by singing Jewish songs in Hebrew. It was a typical reaction on his part.

After leading the Jews to victory Wingate's next exploit was to command a force of guerrillas against the Italians in Abyssinia, which provided him with further experience and the chance to put more of his theories on mobile, free-moving columns into practice. No wonder I felt like a novice sitting at the feet of his master![1]

During some of these exploits Wingate had served under Wavell, who had acquired a great deal of respect for his methods and sent for him again early in 1942. In the previous December Wavell had been appointed Supreme Commander, South-West Pacific, which put him in overall command of Burma, and he ordered Wingate to take charge of all guerrilla activities there.

It was becoming clear by this time that nothing anybody could do could halt the Japanese advance this side of the Indian border. More men and more and better equipment were the requirements and at this stage they were just not available.

We could only hope to delay the Japs while preparations went ahead, behind the mountains between Burma and Assam, to bar the road to India. Meanwhile Wingate was spending the last few precious weeks getting to know the countryside and the people, before setting out his plans for penetration behind the enemy lines – the spearhead which was to lead the way back into Burma two years later.

He stayed on for a while at Maymyo and I took him around and showed him the type of country in which he would have to operate. We walked for miles and talked for hours and my conviction grew

[1] In May 1941 Wingate bluffed Italian Colonel Maraventano into surrendering his force of 10,000 to his vastly outnumbered Gideon Force. His success was crowned by his part in the restoration of Emperor Haile Selassie to the throne in Addis Ababa. Later in Cairo, whilst suffering from a severe bout of cerebral malaria he cut his throat and was only saved by the intervention of an officer in an adjoining room.

that this was a man I could fight for. He was not the popular type of swashbuckling hero. One of his habits was to dictate letters as he marched up and down stark naked in the heat, and physically he was clearly not very great. But this did not matter in the least. He had a tremendous spirit which drove him on and completely overcame any physical drawbacks. No one could spend long in his company without realizing that he had this burning fire inside him. With his thin face, intent eyes and straggly beard he looked like a man of destiny and he believed he was just that; I am one of those who would agree with his own assessment of himself, and I think the Jews would, too.

But Wingate had a sense of humour as well as his belief that he was a man with a mission in the world. He could laugh at himself and frequently did. He liked his whisky and he was no snob. If any of his officers disagreed with him, and I often used to do so, he was prepared to listen and to argue. One of his great gifts was the ability to pick the right man for the right job and to bring out the best in him. There were times when I began to think he could read people's thoughts; he certainly had great insight into the minds of others and this helped him to give the right sort of lead to those serving under him. On the other hand his intensity and impatience with vacillation, particularly that shown by some of the staff officers who opposed his views or did not fully appreciate the need for urgency, often led to arguments and bitterness.

However, whatever anyone thought of Wingate and his methods I don't think his sincerity was ever questioned. He was flat out to beat the Japs; that was the task in hand and everything else was subservient to it. He was not concerned if some of the things he did were unpopular: his only yardstick was whether they were necessary. This attitude is not everyone's cup of tea and perhaps it is not surprising that he made enemies. But I never blamed him for the way he acted for I knew that at heart he was the most understanding of men. He believed the way to beat the Japs was to be tougher than they were and he drove himself relentlessly, as well as everyone else, to prove this. He could be very morose and depressed, but he would allow only his close friends to see his distress. I think these dark moods came from the strain that he built up inside himself; yet he would never relax his self-imposed disciplines. The tragedy is that he never lived to see the result of his personal sacrifices.

At Maymyo, however, all this was in the future. After I had shown Wingate as much as I could of the surrounding area he said he would like to visit General Slim (later Sir William Slim and Viscount Slim), who was then in command of Burma Corps and had his headquarters north of Prome. We went down by truck and Wingate asked if my stenographer could join us. On the journey he would break off our conversation now and again and dictate a note about the countryside. Listening to him I realized I had been looking at it with unseeing eyes, though I had always prided myself I was better than most at assessing the possibilities of a given piece of landscape. It was a humbling experience.

At Prome I introduced Wingate to Slim, who was then a Lieutenant-General, and left them together. They talked for a long time and on the way back to Maymyo Wingate said he had been very impressed. 'Best man, bar Wavell, east of Suez,' was his summing up of Slim.

Wingate continued his tour of Burma, using Maymyo as his base, and he was very interested when Chiang Kai-shek, the Chinese Generalissimo, arrived there to talk to General Alexander, who had taken over as Commander-in-Chief, Burma, in March. Wingate had been given a free hand and he told me he would like to talk to Chiang. Some Chinese forces had already crossed over the border into northern Burma to carry on the fight against the Japs under the command of an American, General 'Vinegar Joe' Stilwell, who had been appointed Chiang's Chief of Staff. Wingate realized that they would play an important role in future operations in Burma and wanted to establish a good relationship as soon as possible. He also wanted the views of Chiang, experienced as he was in fighting the Japanese, on the idea of a long-range penetration force into the Burmese jungle.

Through the Chinese contacts we had built up at the school I arranged for Wingate to fly on the same plane as Chiang when he returned to Chungking. As well as his long-term scheme, Wingate was in the middle of planning various pre-retreat tasks for the small number of guerrilla-type units in Burma, including the Bush Warfare School, and he wanted this work carried on. He therefore appointed me as his deputy and left me in charge during his absence.

It was then that I first came up against the sort of opposition to his ideas that was to become a familiar pattern during the next couple of years. Almost as soon as he had gone several staff officers at H.Q.

started going back on what they had agreed with Wingate over the use of certain units. When I protested I was told that it was nothing to do with me and that my appointment by Wingate had no official standing.

I demanded to see the Commander-in-Chief but was told I – a mere major – could not do so. Finally, in desperation, I wrote an official complaint to Alexander with copies to Wavell and to Wingate on his return. Much to my surprise Alex eventually received my report but by then Wingate had come back and I told him the full story. He seemed to be used to this sort of thing and took it quite calmly. He went to see Alexander straight away and put the matter right in no time at all. That it should ever have gone wrong in the first place is a poor commentary on the attitude of some British staff officers at a time when our country was fighting for its existence.

Wingate was pleased with his talks with Chiang, who had been very interested in his plans and ideas and assured him of any support that he could give.[2] The Generalissimo had been accompanied, as usual, by his famous wife who had apparently been somewhat upset by the air journey to Chungking. Wingate, like nearly every man who met her, had been fascinated by Madame Chiang, and he assured me, with a twinkle in his eye, that her charm had not deserted her even while she was being sick into a paper bag provided for the purpose. She had carried it out with such grace and delicacy that he said it had been like watching a beautiful gesture by a ballerina. Wingate was also full of admiration for the courage of the Chiangs. Their plane had been chased by Jap fighters after crossing the Burma-China border and had sought refuge successfully in thick cloud close to a mountain range. During the chase and the risky manoeuvres among the craggy peaks the Generalissimo and Madame behaved as if nothing unusual was going on and hardly paused in their conversation with Wingate and other officers.

Not long after his return to Maymyo, Wingate was recalled to Delhi. His outline plans had been passed on there and he was now required to write a full paper on what he wanted and what he planned to do with

[2] In 1944 Major George Dunlop was on his way to China to train Chinese officers in the ways of the Chindits when Wingate was killed. He was recalled and the idea abandoned.

it if he got it. He told me later that he spent many days of concentrated labour on his big report, which he finally submitted to Wavell. Then came the weeks and weeks of waiting in Maidens Hotel, Delhi, so that he would be available at a moment's notice to explain any point which the staff boys could not grasp.

Looking back, I have often wondered what Wingate would have thought if he could have foreseen an incident in that same hotel two years later, in 1944 . . . By then Wingate was dead and several young Chindit officers, who had recently come out of Burma after the now famous operation during which he was killed, were in Maidens Hotel on leave. They had been in the Burmese jungle for months, behind the Jap lines and fighting in some of the worst conditions a white man can endure. I suppose they were like any other bunch of youngsters on leave after a battle, outwardly gay and laughing most of the time, drinking hard and trying not to think back more than they could help.

One night in the hotel a major-general started talking to some of them. Presumably he was in G.H.Q., Delhi, where there were plenty of generals, and was having dinner at Maidens. At any rate, he was imprudent enough to say to some of these young officers that Wingate's death was 'the best thing that ever happened to the British Army'. I was not there so I cannot report exactly what followed this remark. It must have been early in the evening and the Chindits to whom he was speaking could not have had time to drink much, for as far as I know none of them actually assaulted the man on the spot. But before the night was out that major-general was thrown fully clothed into the fountain at Maidens by mysterious assailants who were never traced.

Wingate would have been highly amused by this incident; and during that seemingly endless waiting period in 1942 he would have welcomed something to laugh at. For an active and intent man such as he was, waiting for anything must always be hard to bear. In 1942, when the final decision was so important to him and when he was so certain that his plan was the right one and so afraid that others might not have the breadth of vision to see it, Wingate must have suffered agonies of suspense.

Eventually he was summoned to G.H.Q. and grilled by senior staff men on various aspects of his plans. He answered all the complicated questions as if every detail was engraved upon his heart. In the end even the most sceptical officers had to admit that he appeared to know what he was talking about. After a further waiting period Wingate was called in to see the Commander-in-Chief, Wavell, who had been his champion for so long. And at last he was given the go-ahead.

This was towards the end of May or beginning of June, 1942. Burma was completely in the hands of the Japs and Wingate, weary as he must have been after his duel with the staff boys, was faced with forming what had to be a crack special force, if it was to succeed, from the inexperienced battalions.

The magnitude of his task was recognized even at G.H.Q., which apologized for the quality of the material at his disposal. But Wingate, who was a student of the Bible and always insisted on at least one padre for each Chindit battalion, said to me some time later: 'God often gives man peculiar instruments with which to pursue His will. David was armed only with a sling.' Wingate proved with the Chindits that troops not specially selected for out-of-the-ordinary duties can be made into crack fighting units with the right sort of training and inspiring leadership of the type he was able to provide.

At about the time Wingate got the go-ahead in Delhi I came out of Burma with the remnants of my Bush Warfare School men. But much had happened to me in the two or three months since Wingate had left Maymyo. I had tangled again with the Japs in several encounters and barely got away with my life. And when, sick and emaciated, I finally reached safety in Assam I narrowly escaped a court martial.

10

Calvert's Commandos

There is something horrifying about a general retreat. Nothing is worse for morale than the order to withdraw in the face of the enemy. As positions are abandoned communications become more and more difficult, and what facts are available gradually sink under the weight of rumours that cannot be checked. Civilians who have no wish to see their country ruled by the invading troops turn refugee; others are driven from their homes by gunfire or plain fear; and they all join the fleeing troops, often on the only available route. The result is chaos and confusion, both at the front, or what is left of it, and at the various command headquarters in the rear.

This was the situation in Burma in the spring of 1942. As the Japs advanced, thousands of British and Commonwealth troops, together with Indian and Burmese refugees, plodded along the jungle paths that led to the mountains around Assam, the Indian border State. Many were wounded, sick and hungry. And many of them marched for hundreds of miles before they reached safety at Imphal.

General Alexander, with Wavell's full approval, had as his main objective the evacuation of as many troops as possible so that a new defence line could be built in strength to defend India from the triumphant Japs. Clearly, everything possible had to be done to delay and harass the enemy to give our main force more time to get out, and Alex ordered me to form a special unit to help to do this. I was to use what was left of my Bush Warfare School staff as a nucleus – that was five officers and seventeen other ranks – and recruit the other officers and men wherever I could find them.

I ended up with several hundred chaps from convalescent camps, hospitals, offices, transport units which had lost their transport, signals, military police and even some deserters serving their time in a detention camp. We were a real odds-and-sods outfit which became known by all sorts of names from the rather formal Bush Warfare Battalion to the more personal 'Calvert's Commandos'.

It was a mad business, with little time for organization before we were sent off to hold the vital Gokteik Viaduct about thirty miles east of Maymyo. The intention was to hold down the Japs on the other side of it as long as we could and keep them off the backs of the retreat. I was under no illusion about the difficulty of leading strange, half-trained troops, many of them pretty wild, into a scrap with the well-disciplined and battle-hardened enemy forces that were leading the advance. And just before our first clash with the Japs my worst fears were justified.

I was making my nightly round of our positions and called in on a company formed from men out of the convalescent camps and detention barracks. They were in a complete shambles. Some of the sentries were asleep. And, worst of all, six other sentries had stolen a truck and disappeared. I was hopping mad but almost at once I heard shots not far away, and had to devote the next hour or so to beating off an attack on one of our flanks by a strong Jap patrol.

While the fighting was going on I kept thinking what might have happened if the enemy had chosen to come at us on the flank guarded by the crowd I had just seen. The Japs could have got right into the middle of our position and blown hell out of us almost before we knew they were there. In my mind's eye I could see the dead and the wounded and I decided that I would go out and search for the men who had run away and left a gap in our defences, which could so easily have brought death and suffering to their comrades.

As soon as we had beaten off the Japs I set out, with a few of my own men to help me. We hunted around for several hours but it was a hopeless task. The runaways had had a good start and made the most of it. We returned without finding them and I never saw or heard of the men again, although I reported the incident and made enquiries later. They may have found their way to Imphal and returned to their units, or joined new ones, without ever mentioning they had been with me; no one would have bothered to question them closely at that confusing time. Or they may have wandered into a Jap patrol and been killed or taken prisoner.

The story got around that I not only went out after them but found them and killed them for their cowardice. That is not true. But I was in a cold fury at the way they had exposed us all to danger and defeat; they didn't know the Japs were going to attack the opposite flank and not the one they were supposed to be guarding. Perhaps it was as well for them, and for me, that I did not find them.

After that unfortunate beginning the unit seemed to take hold of itself. Everyone knew that I had gone out myself to try to find the sentries and even the wildest ones from the detention camp were prepared to follow me after that. I have always maintained that the men in a fighting unit must be led from in front by a commander they know is willing and able to do everything he asks them to do and probably more; I think this particular experience is a good illustration of that principle.

From then on my so-called 'commandos' – a misnomer if ever there was one – fought like demons, though many were only half fit. I remember seeing one man apparently hanging behind in a bayonet charge and I cursed him for not getting at the enemy. He stopped in the middle of the scrap and opened the top of his trousers. I saw a big gaping hole in his thigh, a half-healed wound that had broken open. As he did up his trousers he said: 'I'm doing my best, sir.' Most men would have been out for the count in his condition but he plugged on and played his part. I felt a complete louse.

After about a week at Gokteik we were ordered to withdraw but I pulled my men back reluctantly. I had asked several times for permission to blow up the huge viaduct that straddled the Gokteik Gorge, and every time it had been refused. I was baffled but I gave my superiors the benefit of the doubt and just hoped they had a good reason for this apparent foolishness which, as far as I could see, would only help the Japs.

Later I saw Alex and almost the first thing he asked was: 'Did you blow up the viaduct?'

I was even more baffled now: surely he knew what orders I had been given? 'I asked for permission about half a dozen times, sir. But I was told to leave it alone,' I told him.

He looked put out, then explained the position to me. Apparently there were strong political reasons why he could not issue a direct order to blow up the viaduct. What the reasons were he did not say. But he had wanted it blown up all the same and sent me there in the first place because he had been told I was the most likely person to disobey orders!

It was ironic that the one time I could have ignored authority and got away with it I had decided to behave myself. I apologized to Alex rather weakly and he was very pleasant about it. But he seemed disappointed that I had let him down by doing what he had told me to do.

Soon after the Gokteik incident we were called in to help at several other points, and our numbers began to diminish rapidly, partly through casualties and partly because the pace was too hot for some of the men who were never cut out for this type of thing. I did not blame them; in fact I admired their guts for volunteering to join me in the first place. Many of them had been clerks, orderlies and so on, just as essential to an army in their own way as its fighting men. When it became clear that a bunch of them could not take much more I would send them off with some walking wounded to join the retreat; men like them would be needed back in India to help in the administration of new fighting units, and in any case they would be more of a hindrance than a help to me if they couldn't keep up with the rest.

By now Maymyo had fallen and the British troops in that area were rapidly moving westwards – through Mandalay, over the Irrawaddy via the big Ava Bridge and on to cross the Chindwin river and reach Kalewa. The situation around Mandalay was very confused and I was told to go in and see if anything could be done for people who might have been left behind. Once again we set off in the opposite direction to the retreat and as we moved towards Mandalay troops and refugees on their way to India passed through us, surprised to see the way we were heading.

The town was deserted by the time we got there and was in a dreadful mess, with homes and shops abandoned by their owners and showing all the untidy signs of hasty departure. Most of my outfit had got more or less hardened to the miserable backcloth of defeat by this time, but for some of the less reliable ones Mandalay seemed to be the last straw. I think the sight of all these people trekking towards India, while we were going the other way on what some of them began to call a suicide mission, was also having its effect. These chaps hadn't been trained for this sort of thing and I didn't blame them for the way they felt; on the other hand I was determined to carry out my orders. So, if I was going to avoid trouble, perhaps even mutiny, I had to dream up something to raise morale.

One of the buildings that had been abandoned was the local brewery and it occurred to me that a bottle or two of beer might help to keep the lads in good heart. In the Army there always seems to be someone in a unit who knows something about any job that crops up, from coal-heaving to piano-tuning. In this case it was brewing and, sure enough, we found three chaps who had worked in a brewery back home before joining up, and were willing to try their hand at the Burmese vintage.

The Mandalay beer factory had obviously been evacuated in double-quick time, for these chaps had a look round then told me there were plenty of the necessary supplies and all that needed doing was to start up the machines, which were in good shape. I ordered them to go ahead and rarely have I seen a command obeyed so readily. Soon we were able to dish out beer to the lads. It could probably have done with standing a little longer and maybe there were other imperfections that would have upset the customers in normal times. But at that moment our beer was the best we had ever tasted and, as I had hoped, it did the trick on morale-raising.

There was, in fact, little for us to do in Mandalay after we had put a few stragglers on the right road and told them that we were pretty certain there were no Japs between us and the main retreating force, which was now about thirty miles away. Soon after they had gone we moved off ourselves and left the place to the Japs, who had not shown up so far. Presumably they had either by-passed the town or were having difficulty keeping up with the momentum of their own advance.

We went back across the Ava Bridge, which had already been mined and would be blown very shortly when the area commander decided he could wait no longer for men who might have been trapped or delayed and were now trying to catch up with the rest. I remember hoping as I crossed the bridge that what had happened at Gokteik Viaduct would not happen here; that would be too much of an advantage to give the Japs.

I was relieved to reach the western side of the Irrawaddy. Some friendly Burmese had told us the enemy were getting too close for comfort and we were certainly not equipped to try to stop a full-scale advance. I looked back at the bold arches of the great bridge spanning the river and reckoned that there would be a large hole in the middle of them before many more hours had passed. I had no means of knowing that before those charges went up I would be going back across the Ava Bridge to play a desperate trick in the hope of deceiving the wily Japs.

11

The Plans that Never Were

While the retreat was on there was always the risk of a sudden clash with a forward Japanese patrol, and in these uncertain conditions men on both sides were inclined to be somewhat trigger-happy. For this reason the Burmese who had decided to stay put were wisely keeping out of sight as much as possible. The strange emptiness of the countryside was very noticeable as we moved west from the Irrawaddy, and the village we reached a mile or two inland looked just as deserted as the rest. Suddenly, however, we came round a bend and saw a group of at least fifty women and children squatting by the side of the road, bundles of belongings beside them almost as if they were waiting for the next bus.

They waved cheerily to us as we approached but made no attempt to move and clearly did not expect us to stop to pick them up. Some of them looked weary but they all managed a smile and there was a complete absence of despair or panic, the two facial expressions that had become most familiar to us in those unhappy days.

I was completely baffled and ordered my tattered convoy of half a dozen ramshackle trucks to halt. I glanced down the line of our so-called transport and wondered how on earth I was going to solve this new problem. Trucks had, in fact, been one of our biggest headaches right from the start. The only vehicles we could get hold of were the old and battered ones that had been left behind as unworkable by other units. We would have come to a halt long before this had it not been for my wonderful R.E.M.E. (Royal Electrical and Mechanical Engineers) officer, Captain MacQueen, and his band of magicians. They had no store of spares to draw upon, no regular supply of oil and petrol, but somehow or other, by some fantastic improvisations, they kept us going.

By this time, however, we were getting down to rock bottom. We had cannibalized everything we could find for spares, engine oil, etc., and there was nothing else to fall back on if there were further breakdowns. On several trucks the petrol pumps were no longer working; Captain MacQueen had solved that problem by roping makeshift petrol tanks on to the cabin roofs and running pipes straight into the carburettors. It was by no means a perfect arrangement, for it wasted fuel, apart from anything else. But we felt we could carry on for a while because we had discovered an abandoned store of R.A.F. 100-octane spirit in Mandalay and loaded as much as we could carry on to the trucks. This made the journey more cramped and uncomfortable than ever for the men, but at least it meant they did not have to walk. The point was that while we were mobile we could be of some practical use; once the trucks packed up there would be little we could do but join the retreat with the rest.

I felt all this weighing heavily on my mind as I stood at the roadside and looked at the calm and collected group of women and children gathered there. Some were Burmese, some Anglo-Burmese, others probably Anglo-Indian and a few British. The majority of them, I discovered, were housekeepers, domestic servants and so on, and several of the children belonged, in fact, to their employers. Some had been parted from their households in the general chaos of evacuation, others had been told to wait to be picked up and nothing had arrived for them. Most of them had no idea whether their employers or their families were now dead or alive and the cool way in which they were facing what could easily have been the end of the world for them was quite magnificent.

I got my information from a very nice but clearly very firm and decided grey-haired lady of about sixty-five. I think she was British but she had obviously spent a long time in Burma and at times it is difficult to tell in these cases whether or not there is a touch of Burmese or Indian. As she spoke to me, standing straight and erect and amazingly well groomed under the circumstances, it became clear that it was she who had gathered the group together and kept them calm and orderly. She seemed to think there was nothing unusual in this; from the way she spoke she obviously felt that, although they were refugees and close to imprisonment – or perhaps worse – by the Japs, there was no call for unseemly behaviour! She was the sort of person who made me very much aware of my sweaty and rather grubby appearance.

There was one point which still puzzled me. 'Why are you all waiting by the side of the road, ma'am?' (I never thought to ask her name and she would probably have thought it improper to volunteer it.)

'We are waiting to be collected, of course, Major,' she replied.

This really staggered me, for I knew the nearest British transport was miles away by now and heading towards India, not Mandalay.

'Who is it you're expecting?' I asked carefully.

She named the colonel of a unit which, she said, had moved out several days before. Her attitude said clearly that if a senior British officer promised he would arrange for women and children to be picked up he would keep his word, and I had no doubt she was right. But anything could have happened to that colonel since he had spoken to her. He might have tangled with a Jap patrol and be dead; or he might have caught up with the retreat and demanded trucks to return for these people, and been told there were no trucks available. When the colonel made his promise I had no doubt he meant to keep it and had done everything in his power to do so. I was also sure that no trucks would be on their way to pick up these people.

'I think it might be as well if you went along in some of our vehicles,' I said as casually as I could. 'It's possible the others may have been delayed for some reason.'

She was no fool. Obviously she had begun to appreciate at the back of her mind that their chances of rescue were fading as the days went by, though she was still clinging firmly to the belief that the colonel would return. She appeared to consider my offer, weighing the pros and cons. For her, there was a right and wrong way of doing things, no matter what the situation, and anxious as I was I could not bring myself to hurry her too much.

'Where would you take us?' she asked.

'Right into India, if necessary,' I said. 'But I'm sure we can hand you over to a British unit along the road somewhere. They'll look after you.'

At last she agreed that they would go, after I had promised to tell the colonel what had happened if and when he came back for them. We helped them into the trucks and I sent some of the men along as guards in case of trouble. For the rest of us there was nothing for it but to wait until the trucks came back. I reckoned they would be away about twenty-four hours by the time they had caught up with the main retreat, explained the situation, unloaded their passengers and made the return trip. Meanwhile I decided we might as well take advantage of the situation and grab a badly needed rest. Our informants said the Japs in this area were still over the other side of the river so I ordered sentries to be posted and put my feet up.

Not long afterwards an orderly ran up and for a moment I thought the man had got a touch of the sun. The gist of his message, which I made him repeat twice, was that a British Army staff car had arrived in the village and the two officers in it wanted to see me. Who on earth could this be? It was no part of a general's job to lag behind a retreat. On the other hand, who but a general could get hold of a staff car in running order at this stage of the proceedings?

My question was soon answered when an old familiar voice hailed me: 'Get on your feet, you lazy old so-and-so, and come and say Hello.'

It was Peter Fleming.

I was delighted to see him. 'I thought only a brasshat could get himself a car to drive around in at the moment,' I said. 'But I might have known you'd wangle one somehow or other.'

Peter and the captain with him grinned and we exchanged further pleasantries before they told me what they really wanted. My job with Peter in Kent and Sussex in 1940 had been a temporary posting for me, but he was still with Military Intelligence and engaged at the moment on the vital business of deception. I assured him he had me completely baffled when he introduced the captain with him, a chap with a patch over one eye, as General Wavell's A.D.C.

'If you take my advice you'll head straight back for G.H.Q. and leave this madman Fleming to his own devices,' I told the A.D.C. 'I was with him in England and he got me into quite enough trouble there, without any Japs about. If you let him take you any further down the road in that car you won't be alive long enough to deceive anyone.'

I was half serious but the two of them laughed heartily and Peter told me to pipe down while he explained the situation. He also told me to think of a chap who would like to be taken for a ride; he wanted two volunteers to help him and he was sure I would want to be one of them, leaving one more to choose. I was not so sure, but I let him tell his story.

84

The Plans that Never Were

The aim of this particular piece of deception was to try to convince the Japs that we were much stronger in India, and that part of the East generally, than we really were. The object was to make them move troops and naval and air units to cover Allied forces that in fact did not exist, thereby relieving the pressure on other parts of the area.

Ever since Peter had arrived he had been keeping a firm grip on an attaché case and he now explained that this was the centrepiece of the whole operation. It belonged to General Wavell. And inside it were a mixed bunch of papers, messages, plans and letters, including several personal ones from the general's wife, to make the whole thing more convincing. Some of the stuff was genuine but it would tell the Japs nothing they didn't know already. The rest, carefully prepared by the intelligence boys, referred to non-existent armoured units and artillery in India and Ceylon, and movements of ships in the Indian Ocean which were in fact somewhere else. There were also 'top secret' messages referring to reinforcements that were on their way east, and I have no doubt that General Wavell wished that the faked messages were true. If they had been the need for the deception might not have been so urgent.

So much for the documents to be planted. The next problem was how to plant them in a convincing manner, and that was where Wavell's A.D.C. and the staff car came in. One or two of the messages in the attaché case would make it clear that the captain had been on a visit to forward area commanders, briefing them on future plans on Wavell's behalf. Peter and the captain were to take the staff car as near to the Japs as possible, then make it appear that they suddenly realized they were going the wrong way, turn round and crash in their haste to escape capture. The attaché case would be 'lost' in the scramble and found by the Japs.

It was in this hair-raising part of the plan that Peter wanted my assistance. I knew the countryside pretty well by now and would be able to lead the getaway, as well as helping to wreck the car. If we were captured it would not appear unusual for an officer of a rearguard unit to be escorting two G.H.Q. officers. And it was because of the possibility of capture that Peter wanted one of my men with us, as it was rare for officers to drive their own staff cars; it would look better if we had a private as driver.

I had little difficulty in selecting a man. Private Williams, of the

Welch Regiment, was the obvious choice. He had been with me at the Bush Warfare School and had more than proved his worth on the showboat raid and other operations since then. At one stage he was captured by the Japs, lined up with some other prisoners, bayoneted and left for dead. But he fooled the enemy by feigning death and escaping later. In spite of a nasty bayonet wound he walked about twenty miles until he found a British unit. And as soon as he recovered he insisted on returning to me. He was intelligent as well as tough and later on, back in India, was made an instructor at a jungle warfare school. But he always refused promotion, even to lance-corporal, and appeared on the school staff list among his fellow instructors, all officers and senior N.C.O.s, simply as Private Williams. He was a wonderful type and just the man to take on a job like this.

One other little snag attached to the plan was that the Ava Bridge was due to be blown at midnight that night. We would have to cross it to get near enough to the Japs. And we would have to get back before the demolition deadline if we wanted to avoid a half-mile swim across the swiftly flowing Irrawaddy. Every minute counted, so I handed over to my senior officer and told him to take the men through to India if I wasn't back by the time the trucks returned. Then the four of us piled into the staff car and set off.

Peter asked me to drive as I knew the road (it wasn't unusual for an officer to give the driver a spell) and I had an empty feeling in my stomach as we swept back over the Ava Bridge. The muddy river below looked cruel and forbidding and I didn't fancy a swim in it. According to Peter's information we would meet the Japs quicker by turning south towards Kyaukse rather than north to Mandalay. As we drove towards the enemy we saw odd remnants of battered British units on the eastern bank heading as fast as they could for the bridge. The sight of a staff car racing the other way obviously deceived them into thinking we were crazy!

About thirty miles or so from the bridge we stopped on the brow of a hill with a good view of the surrounding countryside. We were pretty sure the Japs were nearby so Williams and myself got out, lifted the bonnet and peered in at the engine as if we had broken down. Peter and Wavell's A.D.C. kept a sharp lookout and their yells coincided with a burst of fire from the Japs. Luckily the enemy were too far away to do any damage with rifles or tommy-guns. And our first object had been achieved: we had been spotted.

We slammed the bonnet down and jumped back into our seats. As I started the engine and swung the car round fiercely I spotted a Jap or two breaking cover, but still several hundred yards away. There was a convenient sharp corner and an embankment just up the road, which we had noted previously, and I belted the car into this, going much too fast, then rammed on the brakes. The tyres squealed and at the last moment the plan nearly went wrong because the confounded brakes were so good! I had to ease my foot off the pedal slightly to make sure we went off the road and over the embankment. The car began to turn over very slowly, giving us plenty of time to get out, but it was dented enough to be convincing. Peter made sure the attaché case was not too near the wreck, in case of fire; he threw it just far enough so that it looked as though it had been flung clear on impact.

The Japs had seen the crash and were running towards us. We loosed off a few shots in their direction before diving into the thick scrubland beside the road. Once in there the advantage was with us, for we were comparatively fresh and not lumbered with equipment. We had compasses and where paths did not run the right way we cut through the bush. To start with we heard the Japs thrashing about behind but they gave up the chase after a while. No doubt they were content enough with what they had found.

Our main aim now was to reach the Ava Bridge before it was blown. It was getting dark but we pressed on and made good time and were relieved to see the bridge still intact when we reached the bank. Soon after we crossed the rearguard demolition boys blew their charges and two of the huge spans crashed down into the river. The Japs would repair it, but for a while the number of troops they could move across the Irrawaddy at that vital point would be severely restricted.

Peter and his companion rested for a few hours then went on alone to catch up with the main retreat while Williams and I rejoined our unit. The deception mission had been completed as far as we were concerned; but elsewhere in the area the information passed on to the Japs in General Wavell's attaché case was confirmed by deliberate 'leakages' in places picked by the intelligence experts. Later on I heard that the operation had been successful; the Japs had made various dispositions which indicated they were acting on the information planted on them.

Meanwhile I snatched a few hours' sleep and then our trucks returned and the Bush Warfare Battalion was mobile again. But by now our supplies of food and ammunition were running low and the situation seemed to call for a much smaller unit which could move swiftly and even live off the land if necessary, and in any case the trucks could not go on much longer. So I sent off most of the men to join up with the retreat and kept a small nucleus of my own original chaps with me.

My orders had been to operate behind the retreat, getting in the Japs' way as much as possible and helping any of our own stragglers who had been cut off in earlier actions but had managed to elude capture and make for India on a roundabout route. There would almost certainly be several groups of men like this who would welcome some assistance and the sight of a friendly face. And there were undoubtedly plenty of Japs about to be harried and annoyed. It seemed altogether too early yet for me to leave Burma.

12

Kill, or be Killed

The Gurkhas were in a longhouse that stood on stilts on the outskirts of the next village. They had tramped several hundred miles after being left behind in the fighting in the Prome area. Now they knew they were getting nearer the main retreat but there were a lot of Japs about and they wanted to be put on the right road.

That was the message a loyal Burmese brought to me one night at my temporary H.Q. in the jungle. I immediately sent the messenger back to tell the Gurkhas we were on our way.

Shortly afterwards I set out accompanied by a corporal, with the misleading name of Serjeant, and a private. We took our time and kept just off the path between the two villages because we had heard that the Japs were only a few miles away. We had no basic objection to mixing it with one of their forward patrols but I wanted to get the Gurkhas on their way to safety first. From what the messenger had said these chaps had done their share of fighting already, and were probably too weak to take much more.

We had no difficulty in spotting the house, which was set back in a clearing just off the road. A faint light shone through cracks in the badly-fitting door and through the ragged material used to blackout the windows.

'They may think we're Japs so we'll talk loudly in English as we get near the door,' I told Serjeant. 'They're probably trigger-happy after what they've been through.'

The corporal nodded and fell in step behind me as I marched up to the house, with the third man bringing up the rear. I shouted over my shoulder to Serjeant as we stumped up the wooden steps to the front door and he bellowed back once or twice; we both used some ripe language to make the Gurkhas feel at home!

I knocked on the door, lifted the latch and walked in. The house consisted of one long room and in the middle stood a table with nine or ten chairs around it. I already had a smile of greeting on my face but there were no answering smiles from the occupants of the chairs. They were all Jap officers.

I stopped abruptly two paces inside the door but Serjeant and the private, having no idea that anything was wrong, bumped into me and pushed me further into the room before they, too, came to a halt when they saw the yellow faces.

As I straightened up I noticed the table was strewn with maps and there were one or two message pads. Clearly the Japs had advanced quicker than our informants anticipated; they had met no opposition and had presumably been told that the nearest British soldiers were miles away and heading as rapidly as possible for India. From the shocked look on their faces we might have been ghosts and no doubt we looked just as startled.

For what seemed like hours we stared at each other. They must have had pistols or some form of arms but they seemed too stunned to think of shooting; we certainly were. I suppose Errol Flynn would have killed the lot but we just stood there like statues.

Suddenly I came to and realized there was only one thing to do. This looked like the local Jap H.Q., so other Japs would be elsewhere in the village, off guard, perhaps, but outnumbering us by anything from ten to one upwards.

I said quickly: 'Excuse me, gentlemen. Good night.' Then I turned, grabbed Serjeant and the other chap unceremoniously by the arms and bundled them out through the door and down the steps. Then we ran like hell for the jungle.

About half a mile away we paused to get our breath.

'Christ, that was a near one,' panted Serjeant. We looked at each other and burst out laughing. It was bad security but we felt much better for it. We could hear no trace of the enemy on our tail so perhaps the Jap officers found it funny, too. It's more likely, though, that they thought we were just stragglers and not worth bothering about.

Back at our own headquarters in the next village we found our original messenger plus the Gurkhas, nine of them. Apparently they had just got out before the Japs arrived and hoped to meet us on the road with the news of the unexpected enemy advance. But as we had carefully kept to the jungle we missed them.

The villagers helped us patch up four of the Gurkhas who were wounded but, luckily, could still walk. The other five were unhurt but they all badly needed food, drink and a rest. With the Japs so near rest was impossible; the most we could do was to feed them before starting them on their long trek to India. I never heard if they got there.

We left the area ourselves soon afterwards and gradually made our way north-west. The monsoon was expected towards the end of May and I had no wish to be trapped by the torrential rains. We had heard that Alexander's men were now nearing Assam; it only remained for us to follow them and join in the preparations for the hard road back.

We were still several hundred miles from the border and the days of marching through hot, sticky jungle were some of the toughest I have ever experienced, coming as they did on top of weeks of strenuous action.

I can still feel the wonderful surge of relief when we reached a tributary of the Chindwin and gazed at the cool, swirling water. The temptation was too hard to resist. We were not out of danger yet but we all badly needed a soaking and we had neither seen nor heard of any Japs in the past day or two. I gave the order to strip off for a bathe. The men didn't need telling twice.

The river was at its pre-monsoon level, with a swiftly flowing current but nothing like the raging torrent it would become in a week or two. At this point there were little promontories of tree-covered land nosing their way into the water with sandy coves between them, like a coastline in miniature. I undressed with the men in one of the coves then wandered off by myself. Looking back I still can't think exactly why I did so. Perhaps I felt that, although we got along well together, they might like a few minutes to themselves without an officer present. Or perhaps I needed a moment or two away from my responsibilities.

I walked round a little headland knee-deep in the deliciously cool water then dived in and got myself wet all over before taking a look at my surroundings. I saw that I was in a cove similar to the one where I could hear the men splashing about and shouting cheerfully to one another, but slightly smaller. I also saw that I was not alone.

On the beach, as naked as I was, stood a Jap. A pile of clothes lay near his feet and in my first startled glance I took in the insignia of an officer on his bush shirt. It was the second time within a fortnight that

I had come face to face with the enemy at a completely unexpected time and place, and for the second time we were both too startled to speak. I wondered what he was doing alone in that little cove and then I heard more splashing and shouting from the other side of the far promontory. This time the voices were Japanese.

Fantastic as it seemed I could only conclude that he was out with a patrol and had made the same decision as I had, namely to wander off on his own while his men went swimming. I watched him carefully in case he dived for his gun but he appeared to be listening for something. Then a strange gleam came into his narrow eyes and I realized he had heard my men.

I was baffled. If I yelled for help the Jap patrol would hear me, as well as my own. There were twelve of us but there might be twenty or thirty of them; in that case their superior numbers would give them the advantage if it came to an open fight in the confined cove.

While I was still thinking hard the Jap officer stepped into the river and came towards me. I think his mind must have been working much like mine; he could see that I was unarmed but if he used his gun it would bring both patrols running and he did not know our strength. We were behind the main retreat but for all he knew I may have collected a large band of stragglers. Anyway, he wasn't taking any chances on an open fight which would needlessly risk his men's lives. He preferred to tackle me with his bare hands.

He knew his ju-jutsu and the water on his body made him as slippery as an eel, but I was the bigger and stronger. We fought in silence except for an occasional grunt, and struggled and slipped and thrashed around until we were at times waist deep in the swirling river. It was an ungainly fight, almost in slow motion, for it is extraordinarily difficult to keep balance or move quickly and surely in two or three feet of water. Our breathing became heavier and the Jap got more vicious as he jabbed his fingers at my face in an attempt to blind me. I think it was not until then that I fully realized this would have to be a fight to the death.

I was a trained soldier, taught how to kill with a gun, or a bomb, or a bayonet or even a knife in the thick of a battle. Somehow this seemed different, more personal, as the two of us, naked as we were, fought in the water. Apart from anything else I had come to admire this game little Jap. He had all the guts in the world. He could so easily have called up his men and let them fight it out but he had chosen to protect them by taking me on alone.

Now he was putting up a tremendous show and I was hard put to it to hold him. I pulled myself together. Brave or not, I had to kill him. Or he would kill me.

I was thankful for one lesson I had learned: never to take my boots off in the jungle outside camp. Other clothes can be scrambled on in a moment but boots take time, and time can cost lives. Even on this occasion I had stuck to my rule, which was just as well. I managed to grab the Jap's right wrist and force his arm behind his back. And I buried my face in his chest to stop him clawing my eyes out. Then, as he lashed out with his left arm and both feet, I forced him gradually under water. My boots gave me a firm grip and I shut my eyes and held him under the surface. His struggles grew weaker and weaker, flared again in frantic despair and then he went limp. I held on for a few seconds longer before releasing my grip. Slowly I opened my eyes and for a moment could see nothing except the eddies of water caused by his final efforts to break free. Then his body emerged on the surface a couple of yards away and floated gently off downstream.

I watched it, fascinated, as it bobbed along, face upwards, like a ghastly yellow Ophelia. It seemed hours since I had left my men and met up with this unfortunate Jap. Gradually the training and discipline and will to survive took over in my mind and I forced myself to think straight. How long was it, in fact? Probably fifteen minutes. His men would miss him soon. There was no time to be lost. I turned, waded on to the beach and staggered round the headland. The desperate fight for my life had taken a lot out of me and I felt physically ill.

My men were mostly out of the water now, lazing about in various stages of undress. Two of them were singing 'We do like to be beside the seaside', while the others laughed and joked about how good the weather was for this time of the year at Brighton.

Then my sergeant saw me and ran up to help. The singing and laughing faded out and the men stared in amazement. They thought I had been bathing and resting and here I was scratched and bruised all over and obviously exhausted.

'What happened, sir?'

'Japs,' I croaked. 'In the next cove but one. They don't know we're here but they will do in a moment . . . I killed their officer. Get after them now.'

They grabbed their guns and went off quickly and quietly. They found about twenty Japs, took them completely by surprise and killed them all. There was no place for prisoners at that time; we had little enough food and water as it was and in any case guarding them on a two- or three-hundred-mile jungle trek when we might run into another Jap patrol at any moment would have been an impossible task. The sergeant told me later that they had only just made it in time. Soon after they reached the Japs' cove the officer's body floated past.

Left to myself on the beach I was violently sick. I had never felt so wretched before. I told myself that this was war, and the type of free-lance war I specialized in could be as nasty as the wholesale bombing of helpless civilians in a town. In fact this had been a fair fight. The Jap had asked for no quarter and would certainly have given none. I told myself all this but it did not help much.

Some sensational Press reports have said that I killed more Japanese single-handed during the war than any other British or American soldier. I don't know if this is true; but I do know that I felt like a murderer that afternoon over that particular Jap.

Even now, so many years afterwards, the memory of it is too clear and comes back to me too often.

13

Babes in the Wood

Our situation was now pretty desperate. The Japs had obviously consolidated their gains and were once more stepping up the pace of their advance. The patrol we had met so unexpectedly by the river was one of several in the area and we had to double our lookouts as we moved on towards the Chindwin. This slowed us down, which created further problems, for our supplies of food and ammunition were getting very low.

I decided that I could not expect the men to carry on any longer as an offensive unit. They had done very well, better than anyone had any right to expect, but clearly the time had come to call it a day and I told them that our main objective now was to escape to India, avoiding trouble if we could instead of looking for it. I added that we stood more chance by sticking together if possible, but if we got split up for any reason then survivors and smaller groups should make their own way out. Hanging around looking for someone who might be dead would be suicidal.

We had several minor clashes with small Jap patrols but our bushcraft was pretty good by now and we outwitted them without too much trouble. After one of these encounters in the dark I found myself with a corporal and a private but with no sight or sound of the rest. I was fairly certain they had managed to get away and after waiting for a short while I decided to obey my own orders and get out. The other two agreed and the three of us set off alone.

The corporal was my old friend Serjeant, who had been with me when we burst in on the Jap H.Q., and the private was a cheerful Cockney named Medally. Between us we had a couple of revolvers and a Sten gun, a small amount of ammunition, a few grenades, no food and no water. And Kalewa was about 200 miles away. 'What a caper,' Medally muttered as we trudged off in what I hoped was the direction of the Chindwin, and his remark just about summed up all our feelings.

Our progress was very slow, for the jungle seemed to be alive with Japs. But the Chindwin was nearer than I had thought and two days later, weary, hungry and desperately thirsty, we were crouching in the bush and staring at the swiftly-flowing river which made our parched and swollen tongues ache with desire. We knew that it would be asking for death from a Jap bullet if we let ourselves go and rushed down into the cool, inviting water. But the temptation was almost too hard to resist.

At this point the Chindwin was about 400 yards wide and the current looked fairly strong. I knew I could swim across and I checked with the other two. Medally said he was not much good but was willing to have a go. Serjeant said he had been a fair swimmer before he had caught a mild dose of infantile paralysis; the after effects did not bother him in the normal way but were inclined to restrict his movements in the awkward motions of swimming. It was the first I had heard of his paralysis attack and I guessed he had not revealed it when he joined up.

These answers made me think again and I strained my eyes to see as far along the river bank as I could without breaking cover. It was then that I spotted a dilapidated-looking rowing boat tied to a post a couple of hundred yards away from us downstream. It was very low in the water but at least it was still afloat and might get us across to the other side. As we discussed the chances of reaching the boat without the Japs seeing us it suddenly began to rain and in no time at all was pouring down; the monsoon had arrived a little before time. The rain was deliciously cool on our hot and wasted bodies and we just lay back and let it run over us. We tried to catch some to drink and it helped a little but our thirsts were so monumental that we knew it would take those Chindwin waters to quench them.

However, the rain freshened us up and we decided to make a dash for the boat. Much to our surprise we reached it without raising a single Jap. They must have been sheltering from the rain, which was now sheeting down and cutting visibility, a great asset to us.

There were oars in the boat but it was obvious from its depth in the water that it had been holed by our troops to prevent the Japs using it.

I approved of their zeal in principle, though I wished in practice that they had missed this particular target. However, there was no time to mend it and standing around baling out would have been asking for trouble. We would just have to pile in and hope for the best.

About ten minutes later we were back in hiding on the bank, somewhat wetter than we had been when we started. The boat had sunk almost at once and we had to swim back. Again we were lucky and the Japs neither saw nor heard us, though we made quite a splash when the boat finally went under.

'I'm afraid there's nothing for it. We'll have to swim,' I told Serjeant and Medally. 'We'll take off most of our clothes and put them in one pack. I'll take that and you get yourselves across. We'll make it all right.'

I hoped I sounded confident, though in fact I wasn't so sure. The current looked very nasty. But there was no choice.

We wrapped two revolvers, some ammunition and one or two grenades inside the bulk of our clothing and shoved the bundle into a large pack together with our boots. Outside I tied our empty water bottles for buoyancy and we waded into the Chindwin. When we were up to our necks we paused and ducked down and drank our fill with just the tops of our heads showing rather like hippopotamuses. We had decided to do this because a long trek faced us on the other side and the more water we could take in the better.

I set off swimming at an easy pace towing the pack; I am pretty fair in the water after my water polo days and found it no great strain, but the others were not so happy. Medally had decided to go the whole way on his back, which was easier swimming and quite a good idea. The trouble was he kept his head well back and could not see where he was going, so I had to keep him on a straight course. Once or twice when I took my eye off him he turned a full circle and started heading back the way we had come. But at least he was keeping afloat and looked as if he would reach the other side.

Serjeant, however, was obviously finding it very hard going. He was pushing ahead very bravely, swimming a sort of side stroke, but about halfway across he said in a matter-of-fact tone of voice: 'Sorry, sir, I can't go on.'

I called out to him to hang on for a moment until I could reach him and told Medally he would have to guide himself from now on while I helped the corporal. Poor Serjeant was just about finished so I gave him the pack to hold, got him under the armpits and hauled him along. Unfortunately I must have ducked him once or twice for he let go of the pack, which had rapidly lost what little buoyancy it had as everything in it became waterlogged. I saw it bobbing up and down a few yards away, then it finally sank. I could not let go of Serjeant to dive after it so I kept on swimming, trying hard to keep my mind off the fact that we were now without boots, clothes and any form of arms.

When we reached the other bank Medally helped me to drag the exhausted Serjeant into the cover of the jungle, but before we could get there we heard rifle fire too close for comfort and several badly aimed bullets began whistling around. We threw ourselves down into the undergrowth and when the firing stopped ran off through the trees and the thick foliage on a zig-zag course. No one seemed to follow us and I had an idea the men behind the guns were not Japs this time but hostile Burmese with Jap weapons. They would not stir themselves to chase after a few scraggy refugees, so we stopped to take stock.

I had a pair of shorts, a handkerchief and 1,000 rupees; I was thankful I had kept the money in my pocket instead of putting it in the pack. Medally had a pair of shorts and some wet cigarettes. Serjeant, who was still feeling weak after his ordeal in the water, had a shirt and a pair of socks. We were no longer thirsty but we had not eaten for three days. We were beginning to look emaciated. Supplies had never been all that plentiful during our campaigning with the Bush Warfare Battalion, so we had not started out with much reserve of flesh. Now what little we had was rapidly vanishing. The fact remained that there were still days or even weeks of walking ahead of us, and I decided we had better get some sleep before setting out again. It had been a testing day. We made as comfortable a bed as we could from leaves, covering ourselves with more leaves like the Babes in the Wood. But it was as cold by night as it was hot by day, particularly in our half-naked state, and for the first time I seriously began to wonder whether our particular fairy story was going to have an unpleasant ending after all.

Next morning, still hungry but rested, we started out in the general direction of Kalewa. There was no clear-cut route to follow but I had kept an eye on the stars and the sun also helped to keep us roughly pointed the right way. At first we stuck to the jungle, thinking we would avoid Japs and hostile Burmese that way, but the ground soon became too prickly and uneven for our bare feet. We turned on to the next path we came to and the going became much easier. Every Burmese conscientiously removes thorns from a path as he walks along, obeying some unwritten social law, so apart from some uneven patches of ground, where rocks and stones were sharp and hot beneath our feet, we did not suffer too badly.

Soon we came across signs that other people had passed this way recently. The remains of fires beside the path and patches of flattened undergrowth where a camp had been made for the night told their own story.

'They're almost certainly refugees, but it's always possible a mobile Jap patrol may have come this way,' I said. 'Keep alert and we should see them before they see us. Our only chance without guns is to stay out of sight.'

Then we came across a valuable find: food. A pile of peanuts, no less, which we devoured and almost choked over while blessing the man who had dropped them. It was not much after days of hunger but it sharpened our senses and we searched avidly with our eyes as we walked on in the hope of finding more edible treasure. I also felt a little more cheerful because I was pretty certain now that we were in fact following a group of refugees, not Japs. Soldiers would have left more sign even on the hard paths. My theory was backed up when we found a few pieces of old chupatty some Indian refugee must have thrown away. They were filthy but we ate them.

Our biggest find, however, was a pile of sugar beside the ashes of a fire. Ants swarmed over it but we reckoned our need was greater than theirs and shooed them off. Probably several ants went down the same way as the sugar in the end but it tasted fine and gave us a little much-needed energy. By now we were very thirsty and again the gods provided for us, after a fashion. We found a two-foot-wide puddle covered in green slime; at one end the precious liquid lapped against a cow-pat. We strained some of the water through my handkerchief and took down as much as we could. It was hardly nectar but it moistened our cracked lips and our parched mouths and throats. Better than nothing.

We kept going until dusk though progress was painfully slow. Again we made our bed from leaves under the bushes but sleeping was difficult. My bones were too sharp and they ached even though I tried not to stay too long in one position; the cold chilled me right through. In the morning we just got up and walked on. There was no breakfast to prepare and eat, no water to wash in, no equipment to pack. This was the worst day so far. The path had been trodden recently by other feet than ours and we searched feverishly as we went for dropped morsels of food, but found none. At least it gave us something to do and kept our minds off our plight, though I remember wondering in a strange, detached way how many more days we could survive like this.

As dusk fell that evening we heard voices and sounds of movement ahead. Weak as we were, the instinct of survival took over and we trod carefully as we approached the camp that we could now see by the side of the path. It was soon obvious that this was not a military group but a band of Indians making their way to safety, like us. They were alarmed when they first saw us, but as soon as they realized we were not Japs they welcomed us in a way I shall never forget.

We were filthy, unshaven, half naked and our feet were a bloody mess of broken blisters. But it made no difference to these wonderful Indians. They called us 'sahib', though we looked like scarecrows; they gave us mattresses, laid us down and covered us with blankets. While we rested they cooked us dhal (lentil) soup and chupattis, fed us and gave us sweet tea to wash it down. It was the most marvellous food I had ever tasted, though in other days I would probably have turned it away. Then they left us to sleep, a deep, warm, glorious sleep. I had almost forgotten the pure pleasure of it.

Next morning we discovered that these were Oriya Indians from the province of Orissa, south-west of Bengal. They were common enough in Burma for they worked on contract as coolies on the Burma Railways. Having made their pile they then returned home to their families. They were one of the close-knit communities which abound in India, but they took us in and cared for us like brothers. The day before they had been raided by an enemy patrol. The Japs had made them give up their money and forced the women to part with some of the crude jewellery they valued. The patrol commander had also warned them that the penalty for helping the British was death. When I heard this I said immediately that we would go but the Oriyas would have none of it. The sahibs were not well, they said, and insisted that we go along with them.

I sometimes think of these Oriya coolies when I hear talk of the oppression suffered by the Indians under the British and how much we were hated. These people need not have helped us. We were unarmed and physical wrecks. They knew we were part of the great British Army which was being ignominiously kicked out of Burma by the all-powerful Asian nation to which, by all the laws of logic and nature, they were more closely tied. They may have guessed that this was the beginning of the end of the British Empire. But their insistent offers of help were instantaneous and open-hearted. We were at that moment poorer and weaker than they were, entirely dependent upon them, and they could have had no thought of gain. Yet they risked their lives, and the lives of their womenfolk, to help us, the 'hated' British.

They made one stipulation: that we should dress as women to hide our colour and our beards. It was the least we could do so we put on clean sheets and sandals and walked slowly along with them. The three of us had not kept up much of a pace on the previous few days, but we had certainly moved faster than the Oriyas. They were not only carrying all their belongings, including trunks, mattresses, bedding, cooking utensils and so on; they were also carrying their old men and women on their shoulders. With these heavy loads their tread was measured and careful and we made about six miles a day. It was easy going for us and with regular food and drink our strength began to return.

The Japs had occupied some of the villages on the way and while it was impossible to avoid them completely with a clumsy party such as ours we made a point of skirting them and not inviting trouble by going slap through the middle of the enemy. It was an eerie feeling to walk slowly along knowing that the Japs were watching us for the least suspicious movement. Our sheets restricted our field of vision but an occasional glimpse of an enemy sentry a few yards away was quite enough for me. I wanted to run like hell and it took a lot of self-control for the three of us to stay in pace with the Oriyas' careful gait. Medally kept up a running commentary all the time: 'What a lark, what a lark, wait till I tell my old dad, what a lark.' These mutterings were one way of letting out the tension.

Of course, there was always the chance that the Japs would decide to raid us anyway, whether or not they suspected there were British refugees in the party. I told Medally and Serjeant that we would keep up our part as Oriya women and run screaming into the jungle, presumably to defend our honour. Once in the bush we would fling off the sheets and hope to lose the Japs by speed, cunning and bushcraft. It was a desperate plan for a desperate occasion. Thank goodness, we never had to put it into practice.

After a few days with the Oriyas we were feeling much stronger and decided that we could now leave them and make faster time to Kalewa by ourselves. We thanked them warmly for all they had done for us and despite their protests I insisted that they should have most of my 1,000 rupees. With much embracing we left them and I never saw them again. I tried to make some provision for them later but Kalewa was evacuated before they arrived.

Two years afterwards, when I was back in Burma with the second Chindit campaign, a band of about eighty Oriya coolies who had been held by the Japs got away and came over to work for us. I told the story of my escape from Burma to my Brigade H.Q. and this ensured that they were well looked after. They did great work as stretcher-bearers and general orderlies and I was pleased to have the chance to repay something of my debt to these people. But for the Oriyas I would probably not have been alive to take part in the Chindit campaigns, or to write this story.

14

Unfit for Heroes

We kept our disguises after leaving the Oriyas and it is not difficult to imagine the stir we caused among the British troops in Kalewa when we arrived dressed as Indian women. The 17th Division was still there and the officers at H.Q. decided this was too good a chance to miss. There was little enough to laugh at in those days.

So, with Medally and Serjeant, I was marched along to where the worried divisional commander, Major-General D.T. Cowan, was at work. The intelligence officer escorted us and he made his report to the general.

'I've got some women here to see you, sir,' he said, keeping a perfectly straight face.

Cowan glanced up briefly then went back to the papers on his desk. 'I'm too busy to see any women,' he growled.

The intelligence officer was not put off.

'I thought you might be interested in their identities, sir. Perhaps if they took off their veils . . .'

By now Cowan realized something odd was going on and looked up sharply just as we were unmasking.

'Calvert!' He looked amazed. 'What the hell have you been doing? We thought you were dead.'

'Not quite, sir,' I said, 'though we came pretty close to it.' I gave a brief account of the later activities of the Bush Warfare Battalion and of our escape and was relieved to hear that most of my men, including Peter Stafford and another friend, Captain George Dunlop, had got out. Most of them had now gone up to Tamu and on to Imphal in Assam and Dunlop, who was very sick, had probably been sent back further into India. It was a route I was soon to take along with the rest of the British and Indian troops who, having escaped the Japs, had now to plough their way over slippery mountain tracks for day after day as the monsoon began in earnest.

Before I left Kalewa, however, I went down the Chindwin with a few volunteers in a last attempt to collect stragglers. We used a small motor-boat and kept going until we were fired on by a group of Japs on the river bank. We then turned round and headed back for base, chased for a while by the Japs until our little engine could build up enough momentum to outpace them. In the end we picked up a few Indians (not the Oriyas, unfortunately) but no troops.

From Kalewa my journey back into India was miserable and depressing, but no more so than thousands of others and the picture has been painted several times before. I suppose, basically, we were all thankful just to be alive. However, there was one unpleasant incident at Imphal which made me feel I would have been better off never to have escaped at all.

While we were waiting to move down to Ranchi, in Bihar, I received a surprise message to report to a senior staff officer at one of the temporary headquarters. As I made my way there I wondered what the call was about. The special jobs assigned to me by Alexander and Wingate were now finished. Burma was behind us and after we had recovered our strength presumably fresh tasks would be assigned in an effort to get back our lost territory. What, then, could be wanted of me now? Was I in trouble again? In an effort to cheer myself up I tried to work out a suitable reply after being told I was to be decorated for valiant work during the retreat. Somehow the words wouldn't come and I was not surprised; I had trodden on too many toes for such things to happen to me.

The staff officer concerned was one of the worst sort, the kind of chap who looks as if he never smiles and could never unbend enough even to try. I should think he was extremely efficient in his desk job. But I disliked him on sight.

His first words, in the clipped, all-on-one-note voice of the admin. man, were: 'Well, Calvert, no doubt you know why I want to see you. On reflection, I imagine you must have appreciated that your conduct was disgraceful and that normally this sort of thing would automatically lead to a court martial.'

I could hardly believe my ears. What on earth was the man

talking about? Whatever it was he seemed to be several stages ahead of me.

'I . . . I don't know what you mean, sir,' I said weakly. I felt quite shattered.

'Come, come, man.' To him this was an obvious and rather silly lie. 'Don't let's beat about the bush.'

For the next minute or two we went on getting nowhere and I never did discover what it was I was supposed to have done wrong. The staff officer grew more and more impatient and clearly came to the conclusion that I was refusing to own up to whatever crime he had in mind in case the admission could be used in evidence against me. In fact I was shocked and dazed and probably rather incoherent.

'This is just wasting time.' He sounded completely exasperated. 'The point is that General Slim says you have done a good job and therefore we are taking no action. I called you in to let you know that the matter is now at an end. That is all.' I stood up and walked out, still not quite believing what I had heard. Obviously some unfavourable reports had been made about me and these had been followed up by enquiries, including one to Slim. I should have been informed about this and the grim-faced staff officer clearly believed that I had been and was deliberately playing dumb. It was possible that messages which should have reached me had not done so in the shambles of the retreat; not only possible, but highly likely. Although this would explain some of the mystery I was still annoyed that I had been made to look a fool. However, I have always believed in looking on the bright side of things, and in this case there was certainly a silver lining: the court martial that had presumably been hanging over me for this unknown offence was now off because of Slim's intervention. I thought back to Wingate's approval of Slim and silently added mine to it.

Most of us were still suffering from weakness and fatigue and I did not worry myself too much about this incident after the first shock had worn off. It was therefore some time before a possible solution to the puzzle occurred to me. The six sentries! The men who had run away at the Gokteik Viaduct before the Japs attacked. I had gone out after them and failed to find them. But twist that a little and it becomes this: 'Calvert was furious and went out after them but he came back without them. He *said* he couldn't find them, but what do you think?' There had been little loyalty among some of the detention-barrack crowd who had fought under me at Gokteik and this sort of rumour would be an easy one to start. Unfortunately, mud so often sticks and this piece stuck for years. On the second Chindit campaign in 1944 I overheard one of my corporals talking to his men during training. He told them: 'This Calvert's all right but he's tough and he won't stand no nonsense. If you don't fight he's likely to shoot you. He knocked off some blokes who ran out on him a couple of years ago, so don't say you haven't been warned.'

Such is fame! Goodness knows how often that story has been told or how much it has been twisted. I think it was a fair guess that it was behind the unpleasant interview I had in Imphal. Perhaps they would even have gone ahead with the court martial if they could have found any proof. But how could they find proof of something that never happened? My conscience is clear, though I've no doubt the story is still told with relish over a few pints when the boys get together.

This incident, in fact, was the beginning of a pretty bad period, the kind one would like to forget but which is remembered every so often with disconcerting clarity. I don't know what we all expected when we came out of Burma. It was enough, during the latter stages of the retreat, to know that the haven of India was near, good, solid India, damned hot and smelly sometimes, perhaps, but friendly in the main and free of Japs. And what a welcome we would get from the British people there! The sort of welcome that would make one determined to get well again quickly and hurry back into the fight. Unfortunately, and I suppose inevitably, it didn't work out quite like that.

It is common knowledge by now that we were utterly unprepared for the Japanese attack on Burma, that no plan of defence existed, and that the complacency of the British in India was only really shaken when they realized that the Japs were knocking on their door in the east and threatening to burst through into the spacious bungalows, the carefully tended gardens and even The Clubs.

Unprepared as they were for an attack, they were even less prepared for a defeat and a retreat. So the poor bloody British soldier found that when he reached his haven after weeks of horrifying hardships along hundreds of miles of jungle and mountain tracks, the conditions there were almost as appalling as those he had left behind. Tamu, Imphal, Ranchi. None of these places had enough accommodation, hospitals, equipment or even enough food for the masses of retreating troops.

The one thing that had kept many sick and wounded men going had been the thought of India, where they would be cared for and cleansed and cured and brought back to life. All they found were the barest amenities, if they were lucky, and sometimes no amenities at all. And many died in heartbreaking conditions.

I am not blaming the British people in India for everything that happened. They had little idea of what was really going on until suddenly they were swamped with a situation that was already hopelessly out of control. It takes time to change an attitude of mind; the switch-over from a pleasant, peaceful existence to the keyed-up life of a country at war and fighting an enemy on its doorstep is a difficult one. For some it is easier than others. And once the real situation had dawned on these people in Eastern India they were wonderful. But there is no doubt that some ghastly things happened first and that many British men died in squalor while their countrymen lived in comfort a few hundred yards away.

From Manipur Road, the railhead outside Imphal, many of us were moved by train to Ranchi, running for two or three days through the tea plantations of Assam, across Bengal and into Bihar. They were hell trains; no other description fits them. The one in which I travelled had no carriages, just steel trucks with straw on the floor for officers to sleep on; for the other ranks, nothing. There were no blankets and no food. We had cholera, dysentery, and malaria cases on the train but there were no medical or even toilet facilities. The lavatory accommodation consisted of ropes to which the user clung while hanging over the side of his truck.

Looking back it seems impossible that this could have happened to British troops in a British country, but it did. We would have suffered more had it not been for the planters of Assam and their wives. They were great people and they knew they were very near danger now, for their State bordered Burma. There may have been complacency further back in India but in Assam the war had arrived and the planters had risen to the occasion. As we slowed or stopped at stations they threw us food and other supplies; we grabbed them through the truck door. It was an incredible business but we had no thought for that at the time. Life was basic then and death was very near and we had little pride left, certainly not enough to object to being fed like animals in a zoo. It was food, however it was delivered.

107

Ranchi was an army headquarters town, but its facilities were for a peacetime army of a fixed number. Little attempt had been made to extend them to cope with the thousands of skinny scarecrows that invaded it from Burma. From the train we were taken to an open space outside the town and told that this was where we would camp. I asked about tents, blankets, clothes, any sort of equipment or covering; there was nothing, no protection from the scorching heat of the day or the cold of the night except what we could rig up ourselves from old blankets and general junk that some of the chaps begged, borrowed or just pinched.

My own weight, which was normally around twelve or thirteen stone, had dropped to less than eight stone. This was due to lack of food and general weakness, nothing more, and I was by no means a hospital case; I soon came to realize how lucky I was. Some of my chaps had been taken off to hospital instead of coming with us to the 'camp'. George Dunlop, who had cholera, was among them and I decided to go down and visit him after hearing some pretty awful stories about hospital conditions in Ranchi.

Finding George was much more difficult than I thought it would be. The few existing hospitals had filled up long before our train reached the town and since then schools and other large buildings had been requisitioned for the sick. The trouble, as Slim says in his memoirs, was that the hospital staff often arrived 'barely ahead, sometimes indeed after, a swarm of patients'. It does not need much imagination to realize the chaos and suffering in Ranchi in those dreadful days. The thing that infuriated me as I walked around from one squalid, understaffed and insanitary temporary hospital to another was that so many of the British people in the town were carrying on as if nothing unusual was happening. There was even a dance on that night at one of The Clubs I passed on my dismal search. The sight of the women in their smart evening dresses, and some of their languid, pukka-sahib partners, made me see red. It was only the thought that I had to find George that kept me from going berserk and doing something I would probably have regretted later. As it was I kept on my way and finally arrived at George Dunlop's bedside.

The hospital he was in, which had been a school a short time before, was not just under-staffed; that night it was completely *un*-staffed. I looked round the place and found only patients. They were in a bad way. George had had no treatment at all during the couple of days he had been there. But his tremendous spirit had kept him going and he told me weakly that there were others worse off than he was. He pointed further down the ward and I went along to one of the makeshift beds where an airman was lying very still. I looked closer. He was dead.

This was too much for me. I told George I was going out to do something about it and not to worry, I would be back soon, with help.

My mind was spinning as I walked quickly out of that terrible place. I had no plan, no idea of what I was going to do; just a fixed determination that something had to be done now, that very night. Then I remembered being told when we arrived at Ranchi that Slim was in the town; he had come down from Imphal after the break-up of Burma Corps. He was temporarily out of a job but these were still his men, the troops who had fought for him and carried out his orders to the best of their ability. It was then that I decided on my plan: to see Slim.

Looking for him was easier than searching for an unknown captain and I soon found my way to his quarters. He looked tired and thinner than when I had last seen him in Burma. For a commander the fruits of victory are sweeter than for those serving under him, but the converse of that is also true. Although Slim had taken over a hopeless situation when he came to Burma Corps it was obvious that the bitter taste of defeat was still with him.

However, he welcomed me cordially enough and I told him about the so-called hospital I had just left, about the total lack of staff, the filthy conditions, the inadequate bedding, the dreadful state of the patients, and the fact that some were lying next to dead men.

Slim's face darkened with anger as he listened. 'I know all about these places, Major, and I've seen most of them,' he said grimly. 'The trouble is there just aren't enough proper buildings or enough staff to cope with this number of sick and wounded. I keep pressing for emergency help but these things take time. They always do,' he added bitterly.

It was clear that Slim was as upset about it as I was and he offered to introduce me to an army matron who had been evacuated out of Burma and was now in Ranchi waiting for a posting.

'Perhaps she can go along with you to see if she can organize something for your friend, at least,' Slim said.

The matron was a quiet, efficient-looking woman and she agreed at once to come with me. We spent half an hour at the hospital, walking round the wards. We found more patients who had died, apparently without the knowledge of the staff, if there was any staff. We found many men who desperately needed attention. And we found, as always when the British are up against it, a number of irrepressible characters who welcomed us and cracked a joke or two and generally seemed to be trying to cheer *us* up! Feats of courage and fortitude are not confined to a battlefield.

The next hour or two are rather blurred in my memory. All the exertion and emotion and nervous energy that had spilled out of me in those last few hours had drained my weakened reserves, and I was just a bystander. It was as if I was watching a truck run downhill after letting off the brakes.

The matron took the lead. I was in such a state I cannot remember her name, but I know we went on a tour of British homes, taking in one or two of The Clubs on the way.

'We need nurses. At once. Come on, I'll show you where to go.' Some people were dancing, some drinking, some just sitting and talking, some even in bed. It made no difference; they did what that wonderful matron told them.

Most of the women had had no nursing experience, but they could clean and wash and cook and make beds and once they got down to it they worked with a will and helped tremendously. It took months, of course, before the hospitals were working as they should simply because there were not enough trained people to man them. But they were never again quite as bad as they had been that night. More volunteers came forward as the word spread round and gradually some sort of order came out of the chaos.

Soon after this I received a message from Wingate. He had thought I was dead and had only just heard of my escape. Now he wanted me to go to see him in Delhi, where he appeared to have succeeded in getting his plans accepted. I went off as soon as I could and took George Dunlop, who was still very weak, with me.

George went straight into Delhi Hospital and I went to see Wingate. He said he had been ordered by Wavell to form a Long Range

Penetration Brigade. Would George and I join him in helping to train it for a return to Burma? I agreed at once and so did George as soon as we put the question to him. We knew we could also vouch for some of the other Bush Warfare School chaps, including, of course, Peter Stafford.

Wingate told us to get well again before reporting for duty and I went off to Bangalore, where my sister was living, and she nursed me back to health. The horrors of the retreat, and of Ranchi, receded into the back of my mind. Once again I had a purpose in life. It would be a hard road back but it was a road worth taking. And I could think of no one I would rather travel with than Wingate.

15

The Lion and the Eagle

By August, 1942, I had fully recovered and set off to join Wingate's new brigade, the 77th, which I was later to command. The training headquarters was at a place called Saugor in Central India, where there was plenty of jungle to prepare us for the conditions we would meet with in Burma. The monsoon was in full swing and everywhere and everything was dripping wet, but Wingate, in typical fashion, had chosen to site the camp many miles from the nearest road, right in the thick of the jungle.

Training with this human dynamo was tough but stimulating. After marching for miles and fighting mock battles in the thick bush we would strip to the waist in the steamy rain and sit round an eighth-century well, part of an ancient temple now in ruins, listening to Wingate propound his new lore of the jungle. He encouraged a critical spirit among his officers and there was plenty of argument. Many were sceptical of his theories, none more so than the Gurkha officers, who thought that this upstart showman in the fancy dress (he did look strange at first with his straggly beard and his old-fashioned pith helmet) was trying to teach *them*, the famous Gurkhas, how to fight in India. In fact they were partly right. Much as he admired them, Wingate thought that the men of the Indian Army, though individually first-class soldiers, had been trained basically the wrong way for the country in which they now had to operate. The Gurkhas, for their part, never really accepted Wingate's ideas, though they fought like demons in Burma as they did in other theatres.

During the retreat I had had the chance to try out, with my Bush Warfare Battalion, several of the theories Wingate had put to me in Maymyo, and they had worked well. So I was probably more on his side than most at Saugor. But I was still critical of some of the

Michael Calvert in 1939.

Toughening up at school.

One of the last pictures taken of Major General Orde Wingate.

Field Marshal Sir Archibald Wavell.

The vital air link.

General Sir William Slim.

Chindits and American engineers at the jungle stronghold.

General Wingate discusses the next move with Chindit officers.

One of the elephants which acted as supply carriers.

Tea-break in the jungle.

The Ava Bridge across the Irrawaddy lay in ruins.

The horror of war reflected in the faces of Burmese refugees.

A glider landing.

Wingate makes a tour of inspection before the campaign. Calvert in rear.

Wingate at White City with Wing Commander Bobbie Thompson, D.S.O., M.C. (hatless), and Calvert. Jap

Just before the last attack on Mogaung. Behind Calvert is Colonel Freddie Shaw and, by the doorway, Major Lumley (baronet).

'Victory!?' at Mogaung.

Fallen Comrades.

points he made, including the close-quarter use of machine-guns to rake the jungle. This seemed a pointless waste of ammunition to me but in practice it proved tremendously effective, as did most of his other ideas.

The cross between hard physical effort and thorough mental exercise was just the right mixture for keying us up to peak condition. Wingate explained that the aim was to prepare for an operation behind the Japanese lines early in 1943, combined with moves by Chiang Kai-shek's Chinese armies from Yunnan, across the China-Burma border. It was a good feeling to have something definite to work towards rather than training for training's sake.

Among the incidents that I remember well at Saugor was the occasion when a snake invaded our mess tent one evening while we were having tea. Before we could do anything about it the snake disappeared under the floor matting and we decided to leave it there for the moment. We were tired and hungry. So we all put our legs on the table and carried on eating.

Suddenly Wingate came in and looked at us in astonishment; we must have looked rather odd. 'There's a snake under the matting,' I explained. Wingate smiled, sat down and put his own feet on the table. And during tea he showed his wide knowledge of the Bible and great interest in theology by giving us his views on the story of Adam and Eve and the snake. As always, it was impossible to listen to him without becoming involved yourself with what he was saying, and a great argument followed. The details of it were too lengthy and involved to delve into here but the story illustrates something of the exciting effect Wingate had on people. Whether they agreed with him or disagreed with him they could not treat him with indifference, whatever he was talking about. He was a man with fire in his belly and such men are always stimulating and inspiring leaders.

Apart from his beard and his clothes he had his other little oddities. I have already mentioned his habit of dictating letters and orders while striding up and down completely naked in the intense heat. And he rarely drank any other form of milk except buffalo milk. For this reason he kept four buffaloes at Brigade H.Q. and the Animal Transport Officer, whose main responsibility was towards our invaluable mules, used to milk them for him.

One day the buffaloes began to get sick, one after the other. Wingate and the Animal Transport Officer tried to help them, but they had no idea what was wrong with the beasts. Wingate put blankets over them and sprayed them with insecticide in case it was something they were catching from mosquitoes or some other bug. But despite the great care lavished upon them one of the buffaloes died and the others remained very seedy. Wingate called in the Medical Officer, who declared somewhat testily that he wasn't a damned vet and hadn't the faintest idea what was wrong with the things. Finally, after Wingate insisted that he should do something, the doc gave them injections, presumably a sort of antibiotic. These had no effect and Wingate, in desperation, began dosing them with some of our very small stock of Scotch whisky.

Until that moment we had all been faintly amused by the proceedings and our sympathy was mostly for the unfortunate buffaloes rather than for our commander. But this was going too far and the situation had suddenly become serious. We were not particularly worried at the lack of buffalo milk but we were very concerned at the thought of our vanishing whisky.

Then someone had a brainwave and sent for the local witch doctor from a neighbouring village. He examined the sick animals, who were now very poorly indeed, and after some consideration lit a fire. When it was hot enough he heated up several branding irons, seized one firmly, and approached one of the buffaloes. Then he shoved the red-hot tip of the iron between her legs. The effect of this particular medicine, as one might expect, was immediate. The shocked animal leapt to her feet and began stamping about. Unperturbed, the witch doctor grabbed another branding iron and laid it on one of the beast's flanks. He repeated this, with fresh irons, on the other flank and finally on her shoulder. At each searing touch the buffalo leapt about three feet into the air, but she made no attempt to lash out. Finally, after throwing a pained look at Wingate, she started to graze. The witch doctor nodded, as if satisfied with his treatment, and applied the same doses to the other two. None of them gave us any further trouble.

As no one spoke the witch doctor's dialect well enough to conduct an intelligent conversation, we never did find out what disease the buffaloes had or why the laying-on of branding irons had cured them. But we all agreed it was not surprising they did not report sick again and we used to pull Wingate's leg about it.

He took it all in good part and went on happily drinking his buffalo milk.

With his past experiences of guerilla warfare, Wingate knew the value of animals in this type of fighting. We had mules as supply carriers, for we were going to walk into Burma – and, we hoped, walk out again – and would have no mechanical transport. The total number of men in the first Chindit raid was about 3,000 and with us we had about 1,100 mules. During training Wingate continually stressed the importance of these tough little animals until, in the end, we really did like them and trust them; they, in turn, became our willing helpers and rarely showed their well-known stubbornness.

Apart from their main job of carrying supplies, the mules were always useful as stand-by rations if other food became short. This, of course, was a last resort but there were several occasions when it was a question of the mules or us, and we had to harden our hearts. There was, however, one exceptional mule called Mabel. It is difficult to recall just how she differed from other mules, but there was that certain something about her. I have noticed the same thing in other animals, even domestic pets. Some dogs are just dogs and that's it, others have an indefinable streak of character that sets them apart, makes them a personality, and this is often recognizable even at a first glance. The same thing goes for humans, of course. Wingate had that inner fire and sense of mission which made him different from other people. Mabel had a soft look in her eyes which just as surely made her different from other mules. So, hungry as we all were towards the end of our stay behind the Jap lines, no one would have thought of eating Mabel. Our morale was high, even though our bellies were empty, but it would have soon slumped if Mabel had been destroyed for food. We all knew that and she became even more essential to us, a real mascot, and we took her all the way back to India.

Wingate also enjoyed horse riding and eventually taught me to enjoy it, too. I had learned to ride at the Royal Military Academy but the strict and, I thought, stupid methods of the instructors there had put me off. It was something I had to do to pass out, but it was nothing more for me until I took it up again in India. When we went out with Wingate our rides were exciting, interesting and instructive and the horses seemed to react to our keen mood. It was exhilarating exercise, just the opposite to the dull and dreary routines at the R.M.A.

Sometimes during the evening at Saugor we would sit around trying to think what we should call ourselves. We were known as the Long Range Penetration Brigade and as Special Force, and while there was nothing wrong with these names in formal orders and notices and so on we wanted something better, something simpler and crisper that would sum up in a word what we were trying to be and to do. Nothing very satisfactory came out of our discussions until Wingate arrived back from a trip one day and said he had been speaking to a Burmese holy man about a mythological beast, half lion and half eagle, called the Chinthe, statues of which appear in many Burmese temples. Wingate felt, and we all agreed, that the Chinthe symbolized the close co-operation between ground strength and air strength that was the basic requirement for successful guerilla fighting of the kind we were pioneering. It was a short step from 'Chinthe' to 'Chindit', though the name was not really established until after the 1943 campaign.

Now we had a symbol, we had an object and we were fit and ready to go. Christmas came and went and in January we moved off from our training camp to Imphal. The name recalled unpleasant memories for me but I was no longer the half-starved wreck of eight months ago and I pushed them aside and forgot them. On our way to Imphal we tried out supply-dropping exercises with the detachment of R.A.F. transport aircraft that would be our link with base once we had crossed into Burma. The drops were successful and our morale, already high, went up several more notches.

Wingate then had to fly back for final discussions and I went with him. But we were impatient to return to the brigade and were greatly relieved when finally we reached Dum Dum airfield at Calcutta for the flight up to the Imphal area. Several high-powered officers had come to see us off and while Wingate talked to them I checked that our luggage, papers and so on were safely aboard the plane. I then went off to collect Wingate and as the door of the plane was swinging about in the wind, which was quite strong, someone slammed it after me to stop it coming off its hinges.

I found that Wingate was giving a little farewell speech to the assembled company and hung about waiting for him to finish. Before he could do so, however, our plane suddenly moved off, taxi-ing fast to the end of the runway. The farewell ceremony broke up in some confusion which became even worse when, despite the red Verey pistol flares fired by some quick-thinking character, the plane revved up, shot down the runway, took off and disappeared into the distance with all our luggage and papers, which included top secret plans and maps for the Chindit expedition.

The R.A.F. operations room got moving and managed to persuade the pilot, an Indian civilian on charter, that the passengers he was supposed to be carrying were still on the airfield. While he was turning back it was explained to us that the pilot had been overworked lately because of the shortage of fliers and was suffering from nerves. The slamming of the plane door had been enough for him; he had immediately assumed everyone was aboard and taken off. Later I learned from the pilot himself that he had been on the tiles the night before and was also in a hurry to deliver us and return to Calcutta for a hot date.

Whatever the cause – nerves, hangover or both – the chap was certainly in a bad way and we had a ghastly trip. The fact that he had made a fool of himself by leaving us behind seemed to have shattered him completely and once or twice I began to feel that facing the Japs on foot with the Chindits would be child's play after flying with this madman. We had to land at an airstrip to pick up one or two other people and our nervy pilot managed to take the plane in downwind just as a Dakota was taking off in the opposite direction. Goodness knows how we missed it. We took off again without mishap but coming in to land near Imphal I thought we were going to end up in a hedge encircling the airfield. We just scraped over the top of it and when I took a look at the plane afterwards I found a couple of bushes entangled in the undercarriage. A foot or two lower and the Chindits might have been without their leader.

After this amazing flight, which is amusing in retrospect but was not quite so funny at the time, we felt that we were all set and that nothing else could go wrong. We should have known better. Almost immediately a big snag arose. The Chinese offensive from Yunnan was called off because the concentration of their forces had been slower than expected. This news was given to Wavell (now promoted to Field Marshal) at a conference which opened in Delhi on February 1st. General Stilwell, American commander of the Chinese forces, said he would have to confine his activity to patrols. Wavell now had to decide whether to send us in despite the fact that there would be no follow-up by the main forces, as originally planned, or whether to cancel our operation.

Wingate argued strongly that we should be allowed to go ahead and finally Wavell went against the rule book and agreed with him, feeling that the operation would be worth while for the information we would gather about enemy forces and the experience we would gain of long range penetration into enemy-held jungle. It was a courageous decision, for there were plenty of people who argued that the operation would have no strategic value at all without the follow-up.

All was now ready. At the airfield in eastern Bengal from which our supporting R.A.F. planes were flying, three months' supplies had been stored. We were poised at Imphal, with our mules. Then came Wavell's order to move on February 8th. We marched out to Palel by day, and on to Tamu by night. There the brigade was splitting into two for the crossing of the Chindwin, the aim being to confuse and mislead the Japs.

It was at Tamu that Wingate issued his stirring Order of the Day on February 13th. 'Today we stand on the threshold of battle,' it began. And it ended: 'Let us pray that God may accept our services and direct our endeavours, so that when we shall have done all we shall see the fruits of our labours and be satisfied.'

We were on our way in earnest, back into Burma.

16

Chindits go to War

A commando major wearing the badges of a brigadier (Wingate's rank at that time) made sure the Japanese knew he was in the area south of Auktaung.[1] A company of infantry, supported by mountain guns, simulated an attack on Pantha, further south down the Chindwin. While these diversions were going on one group of Chindits crossed the river at Auktaung while others went over in the north at Tonhe. The Japs, we hoped, would be all mixed up by these various activities and as far as we could make out, they were. We were well across the Chindwin with all our mules and supplies before the first clash with the enemy, a slight skirmish with a patrol which they quickly broke off.

The Japs were fairly thin on the ground in the jungle area between the Chindwin and the Irrawaddy and we moved on unmolested for several days towards Tonmakeng, where several columns in the northern group camped while waiting for a supply drop. Wingate was anxious to start offensive operations as soon as possible so he sent three columns, including No. 3, which I commanded, to attack enemy troops reported to be at Sinlamaung, about fifteen miles to the south.

Much to our disappointment the Japs had left just before we got there and we gathered from the Burmese that they had gone off on patrol. We moved only at night, as long as this was practicable, and we found to our surprise that breakfast had been prepared for the Jap officers and men at their H.Q. but they had left hurriedly without eating it. I guessed that they had been tipped off about our presence

[1] Major J. Jeffries, commanding 142 Commando Company and wearing a pith helmet and brigadiers red tabs made himself comfortable in a Burmese village where messengers rushed to and fro bearing signals to his H.Q.

in the area and had set out hot-foot to find us, hence the uneaten meal. It seemed a pity to waste good food so we ordered the Burmese servants to go ahead and serve it – to us. We had a thoroughly enjoyable meal and waited around for a while hoping to be able to thank our unwitting hosts in person. But they did not show up and we decided they must have been having difficulty with their mission. We had to get back to Tonmakeng to join the other columns and could not risk messing up future plans by hanging around too long, so eventually we pulled out. We took with us a horse, presumably used by a Jap officer, and an elephant complete with its mahout, a handy substitute for a bulldozer in jungle country and a wonderful supply carrier.

I always made sure that we carried plenty of explosives with us and as we moved about we mined jungle paths if the local Burmese told us the Japs would pass that way. With the help of my Burma Rifles chaps we also wrote out various signs and warnings in Burmese and Japanese, 'signed' them with the names of Japanese commanders and pinned them up at convenient points to add to the general confusion of the enemy. For example, some of them said: 'Follow this path for –,' the nearest village. But any Jap who took them at their word would have ended up either a very puzzled man or a very dead one.

After the air drop Wingate told me to move south again and soon afterwards came the order to launch the attack on the railway, one of the main objectives of the whole operation. My own column, No. 3, and another column, No. 5, commanded by Major (later Brigadier) Bernard Fergusson, were to advance to the railway and carry out the planned demolitions. In the meantime the other columns created diversions with the intention of drawing the main Japanese forces in the area away from the railway. They made it appear that they were preparing the way for a large-scale attack on the town of Pinlebu and they were helped in this deception by the R.A.F., who bombed the area at Wingate's request.

My objective was Nankan and Fergusson was taking a different route to Bongyaung, about ten miles further north on the railway which winds its way through the middle of northern Burma and was providing the Japs with an excellent line of communication in otherwise difficult country. I had left the main force earlier than Fergusson and reached my target area on March 4th. Previous arrangements had been made to synchronize our two attacks on the 6th, so we had to wait for a couple of days, resting up and taking a look round.

This proved a very useful forty-eight hours. We discovered for one thing that the Japs had not sent all their troops away to Pinlebu. As far as we could make out there were not enough left to stop us doing the job, although they might cause a bit of trouble when the bangs started and they realized we were on their doorstep. However, I was pretty confident we could hold them off without straining our resources too much.

The other news was more encouraging. From reconnaissance parties, and one or two patrols I made myself, we learned that our objectives were well set up and should not prove difficult for the demolition teams. I thought back to my days in Norway, when I had little more than a few depth charges and a box of matches in the snow, and considered myself well off with the explosive equipment we had brought with us into the jungle.

We moved in on the 6th – my thirtieth birthday – as planned, and before the end of the day had blown up two large railway bridges, one of 300 ft span, and cut the line in more than seventy other places in the Nankan area. As expected, we ran into some enemy resistance but I had placed ambush and covering parties and booby traps all round us and the Japs had an unpleasant day. While the demolition squads went about their work the rest of us made it our business to keep the enemy away from them, and I am glad to say we succeeded. Throughout the fighting, which was quite fierce at times, we did not lose a single man, although many a Jap did not live to see another dawn. At one stage a group of the enemy really got the jitters and decided to chance their all in a charge. They came at us yelling their heads off but for some reason we shall never know they chose a spot which meant crossing open country with no cover. Every one of them died.

Meanwhile, further up the line, Fergusson was also giving the enemy hell. He blew a bridge and blocked the line by dynamiting a gorge outside Bongyaung. And so the object had been achieved. It would be some time before the Japs used that part of the railway again.

As soon as the job was completed we moved off east of the railway towards the Irrawaddy. By this time we were getting short of supplies and I sent a call by wireless for an air drop. Unfortunately we were told we would have to wait for a day or two, and it proved to be a very difficult interlude, for the Japs knew only too well by now that we were in the area and wanted revenge for what we had done to their supply line.

We were forced to keep on the move as much as possible, while at the same time not wandering too far afield, and there were moments when I longed for the old days of the retreat when we were at most twenty strong. That is a manageable number when the enemy are panting at one's heels. I soon found it was a very different matter with a column of about 400 men, and 120 mules plus several bullocks and horses we had also brought with us, not to mention the elephant.

I was slightly ahead of the column on one occasion when I began to notice clumps of elephant grass. Gradually the growth became thicker until we were entirely surrounded by it. Normally I would have tried to avoid the stuff, as it is not the easiest type of vegetation to march through, but at the moment I was thankful for the excellent cover it provided. Gradually, as we got deeper and deeper into it, the grass became higher and higher until it was getting on for twelve feet above the ground and each stem was around two inches thick. Being in front with my compass I had to push my way through the tough, sword-like blades that were now quite dense and I was rapidly becoming exhausted with the effort and the great heat in that airless mass. The chaps immediately around me were also feeling the strain and I began to wonder if we had better turn back, Japs or no Japs. Suddenly I thought to myself. 'This is elephant grass. Elephant! And I've got an elephant' I stopped the column and sent word back: 'Bring up the elephant.' After all, she should be used to this huge grass and it would certainly be easier for her to blaze the trail than it had been for us.

The elephant, taking her time but looking quite at home, rumbled up and stopped by me at her mahout's command. Next came the question of communication, for I had no intention of allowing the beast to lead us in the direction she wanted to go; we would probably end up at the elephant mating grounds. So I ordered a corporal who had already made friends with the elephant to get up behind the mahout. We then set out, the elephant first and myself right behind her with the compass. I would shout 'Left, left' or 'Right, right, hold it' whenever necessary, and the corporal would indicate the direction to the mahout by tapping either his left or his right shoulder. The mahout, in his turn, communicated to the elephant in the way these amazing men do these things.

The system worked very well and we got along much quicker with the giant animal out in front. Meanwhile I was studying my compass fairly intently and keeping close behind the elephant, so that when she came to an unexpected halt I bumped into her before I could stop myself. The result was that I was drenched, and while I would have welcomed a shower at that moment this was not the sort I would have chosen, if asked. Looking back, I suppose it is arguable that the whole thing was worth while for its entertainment value, as far as the rest of the column was concerned; it is not every soldier who has the joy of seeing such a thing happen to his commanding officer. As a morale booster it was just right. My own view is that we could have got by without it, but perhaps I am biased. As I dried out it became clear that I would be walking alone for a while and even the waters of the small Meza river, which we reached some hours later, did not remove the stench from my clothes. Luckily there was a change of uniform in the supply drop and I became more easily approachable. But I have never felt quite the same about elephants since then.

Wingate now gave us permission to cross the Irrawaddy and we set off towards Tigyaing, which was on the river. But on the way there we received information via our Burma Rifles platoon, who were invaluable for intelligence purposes, that the Japanese had been reinforced following our exploits on the railway and that enemy troops were at Tigyaing and at Tawma, about eight or nine miles west of the river. Our main aim now was to get across the water and not to mix it with the enemy at that moment. So we decided to slip between Tawma and Tigyaing by night and cross the Irrawaddy a mile or two to the south of where the Japs were.

The plan worked without a hitch, or so we thought, and we reached the river bank safely. Immediately, the Burma Rifles platoon set about collecting boats from the Burmese round and about and in a few hours we were ready to cross. I hated the whole affair and my personal inclination would have been to clear the Japs out first and cross afterwards, but I realized this might jeopardize the operation as a whole and stuck to my orders. However, I was feeling like a cat on hot bricks and there was a nasty feeling in the back of my mind that we were in for trouble. Sure enough, the Japs had spotted us and hit the column just before we started crossing. I organized a strong rearguard while the rest of the men went over as quickly as they could make the boats move, but we were in a tight spot.

The Japs were obviously in some strength and appeared to be bringing up reinforcements, probably from the unit we had heard about at Tawma. We kept them off the river bank, but only just, while most of the column went across using an island in the river as a kind of staging post. A group of Burmese sailing boats appeared on the scene at just the right moment and we persuaded them to help out in the ferrying operation, which gave us a sizeable fleet; without them the situation, bad already, would have been infinitely worse. Finally there was just the rearguard left to go and I decided reluctantly that we would have to abandon some of the mules and supplies. We left some ammunition and medical equipment, which could be replenished by air drop, but took with us our weapons, wireless equipment and demolition explosives, which were not so easy to replace.

We lost seven men in this action and six – five Gurkhas and a Burma Rifleman – were wounded. We got the wounded across the river, which was about a mile wide at this spot, and arranged to leave them with some Burmese villagers. I left a note for the commander of the Japanese forces who would undoubtedly pick them up and said in it: 'These men have been fighting for their King and country, just as you have. They have fought gallantly and been wounded. I leave them confidently in your charge, knowing that with your well known traditions of Bushido [Japanese chivalry] you will look after them as well as if they were your own.' I hoped that this might work and I learned long afterwards that it had done. The wounded men were treated reasonably.

After leaving the wounded we moved east to join up with Fergusson's column, which had stayed to the north of us and crossed the river without mishap, though the Japs were close on their tail. Meanwhile Wingate with some of the other columns crossed the railway and, after some consideration, headed for the Irrawaddy himself.

My chaps and No. 5 column were still ahead of the main force and Wingate wanted to make use of this to retain the initiative we had grabbed by our attack on the railway. So his next order to Fergusson and myself was to continue our southeasterly movement as far as the Gokteik Gorge and to destroy the viaduct there. This took me right back to the 1942 retreat, when I had fought on the viaduct and requested time and again for permission to blow it up before returning to Maymyo on the way out. Permission never came and the viaduct was left standing, a most valuable asset to the Japs. It seemed ironic that I should have been told not to destroy the viaduct when I was actually at Gokteik; and yet, a year later, when I was miles away, receive an order to go and blow it up! But these things happen in wartime.

The task now in front of us was a tough one. We had to travel that 150 miles through some of the worst country in the world, and every inch of the way we had to keep a careful watch for the Japs. They were becoming more and more determined to get rid of the cocky Britishers who had calmly walked into the middle of a country occupied by the Imperial Japanese Army. And they were out to teach these white men a lesson – if only they could find them.

We moved down towards the town of Myitson, and the nearer we approached the more Japanese patrols we spotted in the area. The town itself was strongly held by the enemy but I kept my column in the jungle to the west and by-passed it without incident. We then had to cross the small Nam Mit river and made camp near a place called Sitton, several miles south-west of Myitson, down river. Our local intelligence system, quickly organized by the Burma Rifles, came through with the interesting news that a Jap unit was carrying out a regular river patrol along the Nam Mit between Myitson and Nabu, another town to the south-west of us.

This sorely tempted me. Our orders were to make for Gokteik, and in any case one column was certainly not strong enough to mount an attack on a town the size of Myitson. But this patrol was another matter. We had to cross the river anyway to continue our journey to Gokteik. And it seemed possible that we could kill two birds with one stone by clearing the river of Japs before continuing on our way. I had a look round myself and decided this was a perfect spot for an ambush. I told my officers we would have a go and we were all pleased at the chance of getting our own back for the Jap attack on us while we were crossing the Irrawaddy.

Luckily we had been very careful to keep under cover as much as possible and the Japs appeared to have no idea that we were in the area; marching through the jungle was tougher than using the roads, but it certainly paid off. I picked the spot, as Freddie Spencer

125

Chapman had taught me, where I would least like to be ambushed myself, and took great pains to organize the men properly in their positions. I set three ambushes in line, one leading to the other, and made sure everyone knew what to do and when to do it. The scene was set and only the villains were missing from the stage.

They made their entrance a few hours later, completely unsuspecting. There must have been about a company of Japs, many more than there would have been in a normal patrol. It was clear that they were expecting us to try to cross the river somewhere in this area, or they would not have been at this strength. But it was equally clear that they had no idea we were camped so close to them for they walked slap bang into our ambush, eyes open yet unprepared. We let fly with everything we had and a lot of those Japs could never have known what hit them. It was one of the most one-sided actions I have ever fought in. We simply shot them to pieces. About a hundred of the enemy were killed. We lost one man, a Gurkha N.C.O.

We crossed the river after this but by now the men were pretty tired and we went up into the hills to rest for a day or two before continuing towards Gokteik. Tiredness can lead to slackness and in enemy-held jungle country lack of vigilance can mean death.

Meanwhile Wingate had crossed the Irrawaddy and decided that he would move east into the Kachin Hills towards Lashio, but here a snag arose. Messages from base said air supply would be extremely difficult at such a distance from India; and the Gokteik area would also present supply problems. So, after further consideration, Wingate gave the order to withdraw. Most of what he had set out to do had been achieved by the Chindits. We had penetrated several hundred miles into Burma, attacking the enemy, destroying his vital communications and generally creating havoc wherever possible. There seemed little point in going on if the men's lives were to be endangered further by risking the efficiency of our air link. Obviously the best thing was to go back, consolidate on what we had achieved and come in again, with this first valuable experience behind us. And next time we would come to stay.

My column was now so far south that Wingate ordered me to return independently of the main force. On the way down I had hidden a supply dump of my own near a place called Baw, and made for that first. As we retraced our steps north the Japs were still very active but we reached our dump, picked up the supplies and moved on. It soon became clear, however, that we were surrounded by the enemy, who were now in force along the Irrawaddy and Shweli rivers, hemming us in on three sides, and also to the south of us, completing the encirclement. We had foreseen this situation during our training and we now carried out our escape plan of splitting up into smaller groups, which would have a much better chance of slipping through the enemy. I arranged for a final supply drop near Taunggon then divided the column into ten dispersal groups, which set off on different routes towards the Irrawaddy and the Chindwin.

I took with me the cooks, orderlies and other administrative chaps and our commando platoon, which was commanded by a young Scot, Geoffrey Lockett, a man after my own heart. Geoffrey, who had been a wine merchant before the war, had to have most of his teeth out just before we went into Burma, and he added to the rather grotesque effect of this by growing a wispy beard. Also, he always insisted on wearing the kilt, in the jungle or out of it. He was quite fearless and the sight of this toothless, bearded and kilted Scot charging at them with blazing eyes must have put the fear of God into many a Jap.

With Geoffrey and the rest of my party I set off south again in the hope of drawing away some of the Japs while the other parties of the column got out of the area. Finally we turned north-westward and after slipping across the Irrawaddy without being challenged reached the railway at a spot some way to the south of Nankan, the scene of our earlier demolitions. I still had some explosives with me and decided to use them here to draw the Japs and help the other chaps.

The enemy were being very careful about the railway line now and we knew there were Japs not far away, but I reckoned we could do our job quickly and slip off in the darkness without being caught. I took Geoffrey with me and we laid the charges; then I felt for my time pencils, which would set them off after we had left. These pencils were in various colours, each colour representing a different length of time between setting the charge and the explosion. I had a strict rule that before a demolition party went out they should sort out their pencils and nick them with a knife, so many nicks to each colour, so that they would be easy to pick out even at night. It was an excellent rule, but that night I had forgotten to obey it myself!

I sat on the railway embankment with Geoffrey and felt myself breaking out in a cold sweat as I realized what I had done, or rather what I had not done. To make matters worse some of the lookouts had just reported that a group of Japs were close by; they were an engineer working party building a bridge.

'What the hell do we do now?' I whispered urgently to Geoffrey.

He was completely unruffled by the awkward situation. 'Better light a match and see what we're doing,' he said.

I wouldn't have put it past him to show his contempt for the Japs by striking a match without any cover, but I had no intention of doing this. I looked round in the dim light for a bush big enough to provide a shield, but the banks had been cleared of thick scrub. Suddenly I found the answer to the problem.

'Lift up that kilt of yours,' I said, grabbing a handful of time pencils and the matches.

Even Geoffrey looked startled at this. 'Here, be careful,' he said. 'Watch what you're doing with those things.'

The thick folds of the kilt, held close to the ground, proved a first-class black-out curtain. I quickly sorted out the pencils I wanted while Geoffrey muttered away darkly about suing me for damages. We then crept silently down to the track, set our charges and retreated rapidly to join the rest of the party. We moved off at once, west again towards the Chindwin, for the Japs would be looking for us very shortly and I wanted to make the most of the time the pencils were giving us. Later we heard the distant but gratifying explosions behind us. Geoffrey, walking by my side, chuckled into his beard and I knew that here was a man who would make his mark in the jungle war.

We marched on and it came to me that although I was on my way out of Burma once more, I was feeling much happier about it than I had done the last time. This was not a retreat from defeat, but a withdrawal to renew our strength after a successful attacking mission. We had shown that we could play the Japs at their own game and beat them. A long trek lay ahead of us and almost certainly I would be swimming the Chindwin again at the end of it. But my spirits were high, for we had ventured and we had won.

17

Ballyhoo

Chunks of buffalo meat. Occasionally a piece of python. And rice, endless rice. This was the food we lived on as we hacked our way back to India during the next few weeks. Our beards grew long and we were tattered and filthy. As we marched through night after night, using the jungle darkness as extra cover against the Japanese, we became desperately weary. But it's the odd little things that are remembered years later. Like the Cockney private who, every time the rice ration was handed out, said: 'Turned out rice again, ain't it?' It sounds flat and silly now, but at the time it never failed to raise a laugh.

We got back in dribs and drabs. One column went north, crossed into China and hitched a ride back to India in American planes. But most of us returned the way we had come, crossing the Chindwin between Tonhe and Auktaung. In many cases wireless sets had been ditched or had gone wrong and columns were unable to call for supplies. The R.A.F., however, did a wonderful job and located some of the chaps with reconnaissance planes, then sent in supply drops. And a transport plane even landed on a hastily flattened jungle clearing and evacuated some sick and wounded men who were holding up one of the columns.[1] We certainly had tremendous co-operation from the 'eagle' side of the force.

It was well into May before a final tally could be made with any certainty. The figures quoted in the official war history show that of

---

[1] A party from the Kings led by Major Walter Scott received a supply drop, then laid out the message in strips of parachute 'PLANE LAND HERE NOW'. The next day 12th April 1944 a R.A.F. Dakota obliged and landed. Seventeen wounded men were flown out. Three weeks later the rest of the party made it safely to Fort Hertz.

the original 3,000 Chindits who went into Burma on the first operation, about 2,182 returned to India. The historians also say that some of us marched about 1,500 miles in the three or four months we had been away. When I read that it amused me to think the Navy turned me down because of my feet!

Our reception at Imphal was certainly much better than it had been the year before. The hospitals were ready for us and we were bathed and shaved and tucked up in clean sheets in no time at all. We swapped a few yarns and told the story of Sergeant-Major Robert Blain, a marvellous character who had been at Dunkirk and in Norway before coming East, and was later commissioned to lead his own airborne strike force.[2] Blain had been in my party but I had come on alone across the Chindwin and told him to follow on. He brought our tattered and torn group across, then formed them up in threes and marched them in as if they were at Aldershot. It was a great gesture after all the trials they had endured.

We slept like logs. And we woke up to find that we were heroes. Here, at last, after so many stories of defeat in the East, were some British troops who had gone into the attack, played hell with the Japanese, and come out alive. The war correspondents converged on Imphal and suddenly we were front-page news all over the Allied world. In no time at all Wingate's name became a household word in Britain. And it was during all this ballyhoo that I first read of myself as 'Mad Mike' Calvert. Apparently some of the boys had called me this while speaking to the reporters, and that was enough; I had a new name and once it had appeared in the headlines I was stuck with it.

This was all very grand and we were excited, proud and somewhat flattered at the unexpected attention we were getting. We had always felt that, thousands of miles away from Europe, we were something of a forgotten army and it was good to know we were helping to remind the people at home that there was a war on east of Suez.

But there are two sides to any coin and this was no exception. Publicity and acclaim can taste very sweet to the people on the

[2] Bladet Force, led by Major Blain, was formed to carry out small glider borne commando raids. The first raid took place in March 1944 and Blain was injured on landing, his men going ahead with the mission while he was evacuated. The force was eventually decimated at the last battle for Mogaung in July 1944.

receiving end, but to those who are overlooked it has a different flavour. As I said earlier, Wingate had quite a capacity for making enemies, as well as friends, and there were plenty of senior officers who objected both to his unorthodoxy and to his manner towards them. Perhaps it is going too far to say they had hoped the Chindit raid would fail. But there is no doubt that many of them turned green with jealousy at its success and ground their teeth as they read the laudatory stories and articles in the newspapers.

Back in Delhi Wingate, in his direct and passionate way, began advocating the raising of more Long Range Penetration brigades to be used as the spearhead of a full-scale attack on Burma in 1944. He considered his guerilla theories had been proved in action and could see no reason for further delay. He found, however, that his enthusiasm was not shared by some of the G.H.Q. staff officers. In fact many of them were directly opposed to his plans and it became obvious that Wingate had a powerful opposition to overcome. For a time this depressed him, for he was still suffering from the effects of the hardships he had shared with us and his physical strength, never great, had been severely taxed.

The view is still held by some people that, apart from its morale-raising contribution, the first Chindit operation was pointless. This amazes me. There was, perhaps, some excuse for the diehards of Delhi when they declared that, although the Chindits had gone into Burma, they had come out again and no land had been recaptured. Their case was that the effects of the demolitions and so on were out of all proportion to the effort and manpower put into the operation. On the face of it, as I say, they had a case in 1943 although they were ignoring the fact that Wingate had proved his point: he had shown how mobile columns of troops could move through jungle country as a fighting unit – without relying on ground communications – as long as they had reliable air supply.

But now we know much more than we did in 1943. We know the Japanese side of the picture. General Numata, Chief of Staff of the Japanese Southern Army, said on interrogation after the war that during Wingate's first campaign the Japs had found the territory of northern Burma difficult to defend against guerilla troops. Therefore they had decided 'it would be best to give up defensive tactics'. It was as a direct result of this change in the basic Japanese plan for the region that the 1944 attacks on Imphal and Kohima were launched. This offensive finally failed and the enemy forces were so weakened that they were no longer strong enough to hold back the counter-attacks, which eventually led to the Allied recapture of Burma.

If the Japanese had stuck to their previous plan of stolid defence along the India–Burma border the situation facing us in 1944 would have been very different. In fact the enemy's change of policy from defence to attack has since been described as 'suicidal'. And the Japanese generals who ordered the change have said that the decisive factor which altered their military thinking was the 1943 Chindit operation. This point is made in our own official war history (*The War Against Japan*, Volume 2). How then is it possible for anyone, however much they disliked or disapproved of Wingate and what he stood for, to deny him this great achievement?

However, as I say, none of these interesting facts were known in 1943 and the forcefully presented argument that the Chindit campaign had had no strategic impact found many supporters, although Wingate had his champions, too. The battle went on into July, and it was as fierce in its way as anything that had happened in the jungle. Then another powerful figure intervened, in typically dramatic fashion, and the decision was taken out of the hands of the Delhi staff officers.

In London, Winston Churchill was preparing to leave for a conference on war strategy with President Roosevelt in Quebec, where the subjects on the agenda were to include the future design for the Allied struggle against Japan throughout the Far East. The Prime Minister had heard much of Wingate's activities in Burma and had been impressed with the audacity of the Chindit operation; it had a boldness and spirit which appealed to the great man's sense of drive and purpose. So, at the beginning of August, he sent for Wingate to fly to London.

A summons at that level is obeyed at the double, and Orde found himself on his way home in his bush shirt, with no luggage. Sir Winston has told in his memoirs of Wingate's arrival at 10 Downing Street in the middle of dinner on the evening of August 4th, and of his sudden decision to take the young brigadier with him to Quebec, where he could argue his own case before the men who were running the war. Wingate made the most of his opportunity. He could talk brilliantly and made a great impression on President Roosevelt and the American Chiefs of Staff. At Quebec he also met and worked with Lord Louis

Mountbatten, who was appointed Supreme Allied Commander, South East Asia, the day after the conference ended. At last Wingate had all the powerful backing he needed. He was promoted to major-general, returned to London and began a series of conferences with senior officers on his requirements for the next Chindit campaign, which, it was now agreed, was to be a much larger operation than the first.

For the rest of us this had been a time for recuperation. We had done what we could to help Orde in Delhi, but in view of the heights at which the talking was going on our activities were mainly confined to trying to keep him cheerful. We also went rather mad on occasions, as young fighting men are inclined to do when they have just returned from a scrap. I found it useful sometimes to drop my badges of rank and go out on the tiles as one of the boys. Of course, a lot of people recognized me but it meant they could look the other way and pretend this was just another Other Rank behaving, regrettably, as Other Ranks sometimes do.

From the depths of some of the lowest drinking dens I occasionally rose to the heights of parties at G.H.Q., Delhi, and later at Vice-Regal Lodge itself, the absolute zenith of social activity in the days of the British Raj. What is more, the invitations came to me personally from Field Marshal Sir Archibald Wavell, who was then Commander-in-Chief India, but was to take over as Viceroy in the coming October. In fact I disliked the pomp and ceremony both at headquarters and at the Lodge and sometimes made up excuses not to accept. But I generally went to please Wavell, who seemed to like my company, and we would spend most of the evenings talking in his study while the socialites enjoyed themselves in the big rooms elsewhere.

It was purely by accident that I got to know Wavell so well, despite my lowly rank. While we were preparing for the first Chindit operation he came to visit us at our jungle training camp. Normally Wingate would have taken him around, talked to him, drunk with him and so on; the other officers, after being introduced and exchanging a few polite phrases, would have been expected to disappear. On this occasion, however, Wingate was down with malaria and I found myself with another major having to set about entertaining the Commander-in-Chief in a dak (rest) bungalow which had certainly not been designed for exalted company.

Wavell had the reputation of being a silent man, withdrawn and reserved, who would never talk to anybody. With this in mind I was not looking forward to the next few hours. But I found to my amazement that, after looking round the camp with us, he settled down quite happily in the bungalow, with a bottle of whisky on the table between us, and talked his head off. He seemed relaxed and spoke at length and amusingly about his early experiences in the Army as a subaltern. I think the atmosphere of our simple camp took him back to his young days before he had achieved high rank and taken on great responsibilities. As for his silences, perhaps the people around him in Delhi expected scintillating conversation, which he had neither the facility nor inclination to supply. What he wanted was a yarn with the boys, and he got just that and no more with us in the jungle.

Wavell never forgot that visit. When he heard I was in Delhi he asked to see me and was quite content to sit in his study talking away about this and that; and behind his desk hung the Chindit flag. His A.D.C.s began to realize he could really relax with me and pressed me to come more often. Sometimes Wavell got caught and could not escape from some official party; but as often as not we finished up with a good old chin-wag over a bottle of whisky.

However, when Wingate's call to London arrived I was on leave with some of the other chaps in Calcutta. I was swimming in a pool there one day when Geoffrey Lockett came dashing up with a message. Orde must have felt in his bones that once he could get to the people right at the top he would win the day, for his hasty words were: 'I am off to England. You will be second-in-command 77 Brigade as full colonel and will probably command it.' There followed a list of instructions on what I was to do during his absence, which ended with: 'Get fit and get fat as you will have a lean, hard winter's hunting ahead of you.'

This sudden promotion, and the extra responsibility which went with it, came as quite a shock to me. I was thirty and it was not all that long ago since I had been a junior subaltern, regarding the red tabs of a full colonel with great awe and respect. I was now – for various reasons, some of which I have recounted here – not quite as respectful as I had been. Nevertheless, my swift advancement in rank took a little getting used to.

Things happened very quickly after that. All thought of leave was forgotten and we went back to Delhi to discuss training and planning.

News of the decisions at Quebec came through and I set off on a reconnaissance to find a training centre, and finally decided on Orchha, in the Central Provinces. While the camp was being prepared Wingate came back from London with more officers and told us that six Chindit brigades were to be formed. I was confirmed as commander of 77 Brigade and promoted brigadier, two months after becoming a colonel. I formed my Brigade H.Q. and then my first three battalions arrived, the 3/6 Gurkha Rifles, 1st King's (Liverpool) Regiment, and the 1st Lancashire Fusiliers. During all this time I had been fighting off an attack of malaria but eventually it caught up with me and I was in bed with a temperature of 103 at my first full conference of C.O.s. I told them about the tough training schedule and warned that the unfit would have to be weeded out and replaced by others; sentiment could play no part in the selection of men for a guerilla role in the Burma jungle.

From then on there was time for nothing but the arduous programme of marching, jungle shooting, air supply, air support with live bombs, digging, column bivouac, patrols, signal exercises, water crossings, working with mules, etc. A number of men had to be replaced and several officers, ten or more years my senior, were found to be too old for the gruelling conditions we would meet with across the Chindwin. Without exception they were loyal and courteous to me, although I was so much younger. If they felt any bitterness at being put under my command and eventually being told they would have to be moved from their fighting units, they kept it to themselves. We had plenty of problems and they seemed determined not to add to them; it was an attitude for which I have always felt grateful.

Everything was all very different from our training for the first Chindit campaign. We were so much bigger now, not one brigade of 3,000 men but several brigades totalling more than 20,000. Although the close comradeship of a comparatively small group could no longer be achieved it says a lot for Wingate's special magnetism that he managed to impose his personality on every unit in Special Force. Of course, the 1943 operation had become famous and Wingate was already something of a legend. But it takes a man, not just a legend, to lead and inspire a crowd of tough and highly trained soldiers as Wingate did.

Another important difference was our even greater reliance this time on the Air Force. In 1943 they had dropped supplies to us but we travelled all the way to our targets and back again on foot. One inevitable result had been that the men were tired before we even met the Japs, and although we had acquitted ourselves well we all felt that we might have done even better if we could have cut down the march-in. Wingate had been working away at this problem and the plan eventually evolved for the 1944 Chindit campaign was that we would not only be supplied by air but that most of us would also be taken into the jungle by air.

As I said earlier, Wingate had impressed the Americans, who were always ready and willing to throw in everything they could to help a man with attack in mind. They therefore agreed that a special Air Commando[3] should be formed of Mustangs, Mitchell medium bombers, Dakotas, 100 light planes and a number of light gliders; the aim of this unit was to support the Chindits and the man put in command was Colonel Phil Cochrane, a brilliant and daring American flier. He looked just what he was, a handsome, dashing hero of the air, and a completely different type to Wingate. One newspaperman reported that while Wingate could quote the Bible from one end to the other Cochrane could quote the name of every hat-check girl from one end of New York to the other. But these two men shared the vital qualities of courage, determination and leadership, and they worked together with an excellent understanding. (Later Cochrane and his Commandos were featured in a strip cartoon in America which ran for several years. I never saw it but a cousin of mine who did said I was one of the cartoon characters, 'Dynamite Mike'. Fame indeed!)

Between them, Wingate and Cochrane polished and perfected Orde's new 'stronghold' plan for the Chindits. The basic idea was to pinpoint clearings in the jungle where gliders could make a landing, carrying the advance parties of the brigades. These would clear and prepare a landing strip within a few hours so that the rest of the brigade and equipment could be flown in by light planes and eventually by Dakotas. Rapid defences would be built up around the stronghold, which would be used as a base for further operations against railways,

---

[3] The new unit changed name five times as it evolved, from Project 9 to Project CA281, then to 5318th Provisional Unit (Air), Number 1 Air Commando Force and finally on 29th March 1944 to the 1st Air Commando Group. See the book *Any Time, Any Place* (Airlife 1994) by Philip Chinnery for the full 50 year history of the Air Commandos.

roads, and so on for as long as possible. The landing strip would make supply easier and reinforcements and replacements could be flown in as the wounded were flown out. It was a plan that carried the stamp of Wingate's boldness and flair at every stage.

The brigades themselves were specially arranged and equipped for versatility. They could be split up into eight highly mobile columns of about 400 men each for fast movement, baffling the enemy with marauding raids on several targets at the same time. Or they could be re-formed into a more regular brigade for a co-ordinated blow at a bigger objective. One of the most important lessons rammed home in our guerilla training was to be adaptable and unpredictable, deceiving the enemy with a feint here while attacking there, or better still a double feint while hitting a third target with everything available. Constant vigilance and deception, bluff and counter-bluff, were necessary for success in the sort of free-style fighting we went in for, and many of the casualties were among those who were too stubborn or too stolid to accept this teaching.

Another great feature of the Long Range Penetration Brigades was that nearly every man in them was a potential Jap killer. This was, of course, due to our air-supply system. Most of the quartermastering staff were back at base, answering our wireless calls for all sorts of supplies and equipment by loading them on to aircraft. Criticism of the large staffs we had left behind were made in India by the anti-Wingate boys, who deliberately ignored the fact that if all the supply and distribution staff of any normal brigade were separated from the fighting men their number would have been even greater. This is just one further example of the pettiness shown by some of the diehards who were still jealous of Wingate's success and influence with the powerful.

If we were reliant upon air supply we were equally reliant upon the use of wireless to call in our winged support and to talk to other units in the jungle. Practical difficulties which had shown up during the first Chindit campaign had been ironed out and our wireless system was now excellent. For instance, it is just about impossible to send a wireless message if the mule carrying the set is on the move. The obvious answer is to stop the mule, but the snag is that the chap you are calling up may also be on the move and not listening in. This problem was solved by setting up a battery of high-powered wireless stations in India which picked up messages from units in the field and sent them out to the unit they were meant for when they opened up at a halt.

We practised all this during our training, along with the tough physical work which was so essential to eventual survival. My fourth battalion, the 1st South Staffordshires, arrived from Tobruk and gradually we worked up to a big fifteen-day test exercise under Wingate's eye. For a week after that we spent a glorious leave hitting it up beneath the bright fights of Bombay. It was over all too quickly and then we were back and packing up for the move to Assam, to a place called Hailakandi, not far from Silchar and near the airfield from where we were finally due to take off, Lalaghat.

It was now the end of January, 1944, and for the past month or two Wingate had been involved in tremendous behind-the-scenes wrangles over changes of plan by senior commanders. At one stage it looked as though the second Chindit operation would be called off but Wingate's eloquent and at times impassioned advocacy of his Stronghold policy saved the day for us. The full history of all this has been told elsewhere and it is no part of my story. The effect it had on us was that we went in for a further course of stiff training, including glider instruction, loading and so on, and a fourteen-day exercise of digging, wiring and mining in preparation for the defence of the stronghold we would soon be forming in Burma.

This carried us through February and into early March. Then came the winding-up talk from Wingate in his usual inspiring vein: 'Our victory is already half won, thanks to our training, superb equipment, good communications and singleness of purpose.' And finally: 'There will be no rest, no leave, no return until the battle has been won.'

18

Birthday Party

We were in the air, but only just. The build-up had to be fast, so each Dakota tug plane was hauling two heavily loaded gliders behind it. I listened to the Dak ahead straining its heart out as we circled slowly under a brilliant full moon, gaining height to get us across the 7,000-foot hills along the Assam-Burma border. It was March 5th, 1944, and in a few hours' time I would be thirty-one, if I lived that long.

We were heading for a clearing in the jungle that was to be our first stronghold. We called it Broadway. It was between the railway, our first target, and the Irrawaddy river to the east. As far as we knew there were no enemy forces in the immediate area to oppose our landing, but we could not tell for sure. I hoped for the best, because it was going to be difficult enough landing on that patch of ground surrounded by trees without the added hazard of enemy fire to greet us.

The thought of action is so often more difficult to bear than the action itself and I found this was more than ever true now that I had 3,000 men to look after as well as myself. Apart from that, my nerves had already been stretched a few hours before back at Lalaghat, when it had seemed for a time as if the whole Chindit operation would have to be called off literally at the eleventh hour.

Originally my brigade was going to land on two clearings, Broadway and another one a few miles further south which I had named Piccadilly. Once this decision had been taken Wingate had ordered that no reconnaissance planes should fly over the area for fear of arousing enemy suspicions. On the afternoon of March 5th, however, one of Cochrane's boys carried out a quick recce and came back with his aerial photographs just as we were preparing to fly off.

Quite a party had collected at Lalaghat, including Slim – now a Field

Marshal and Commander of 14th Army, of which the Chindits were a part – and Air Marshal Sir John Baldwin, Commander of 3rd Tactical Air Force. There had been tremendous activity all day, with tow-lines being hitched up, gliders being loaded with supplies and mules, and all the apparent chaos which normally attends the movement of a large body of troops. Finally everything was more or less ready and I was having last-minute discussions with Wingate, Phil Cochrane and his joint commander, Colonel John Allisson, who was coming with us in one of the gliders to take charge of the fly-in arrangements on the spot.

It was at this dramatic moment, with everyone keyed up and ready to go, that the aerial photographs arrived. They showed that Broadway was clear, but Piccadilly had been blocked by tree trunks; no gliders would land there that night. The general opinion was that the Japs had realized the possibilities of Piccadilly as a landing area and had deliberately blocked it, though some time later we discovered that the explanation was much simpler: Burmese woodmen had laid out their trees to dry in the clearing.

Everyone went into a huddle to discuss this disastrous new development and Wingate, after talking to Slim, came over to me. 'Well, Mike,' he said, 'I leave the decision to you. Do you want to go on?' I replied: 'Definitely, yes.'

At this Wingate returned to the group of senior officers. Soon afterwards he came back with the new plan they had worked out, which involved a third clearing called Chowringhee, destined to be the landing place for another Chindit brigade, 111. Wingate suggested that instead of going into Broadway and Piccadilly I should now take 77 Brigade to Broadway and Chowringhee. 'Are you prepared to do it?' he asked. 'If we don't go now I don't think that we shall ever go as we should have to wait for the moon and the season is already late. Slim and the airmen are ready to go on now that everything is ready. What do you think?' He then said something that was typical of Wingate and, to my mind, gives the clue to his greatness as a fighting commander. He said: 'I don't like ordering you to go if I am not going myself. At the moment I have told them that I will consider it, because I want to hear your views.'

I had been having a discussion with my own officers, including Colonel Claud Rome, my invaluable second-in-command. We had taken into account that Chowringhee was to the east of the Irrawaddy, while Broadway was west of the river. I told Wingate: 'I don't want to split my brigade either side of the Irrawaddy. I am prepared to take all the brigade into Broadway alone and take the consequence of a slower build-up.' Wingate accepted this and at that moment Slim came up and asked me what I thought. I told him what I had already told Wingate and I now had Cochrane and Allisson on my side as well; they feared it would be too difficult to re-brief their air-crews for Chowringhee in the time available that night. So the final decision was taken: it was to be Broadway alone. I was as nervous as blazes, I imagine we all were, but we all knew we had to go. We were 77 Brigade, Wingate's Brigade, and it was up to us to lead the way. In any case Broadway was clear and I could really see no reason why we should not go in there just because Piccadilly was blocked. This type of operation was always risky; it was now slightly more so, but not enough to call it off.

My stomach felt distinctly queasy as we bumped and swayed over the mountains in the flimsy wooden glider. A lot of the others had dozed off but my mind was buzzing and I couldn't sleep. I glanced up and found reassurance in the calm figure of my American glider pilot, an unshakeable character called Lees. I had seen him at work during training and when Phil Cochrane asked me if I wanted anyone in particular to pilot my glider I had asked for Lees. I was glad of it now. With his experience he knew better than most just how difficult it was going to be to put his glider down in a jungle clearing in the dark, but he was sitting up in front there chewing gum slowly and looking quite unconcerned. What a balm a chap like that can be to a worried and harassed commander!

I looked through my peephole and saw that we were close to the Chindwin. It gleamed below us in the moonlight and although I was not swimming across it this time I almost wished that I was still the leader of a small band of odds-and-sods, wandering more or less as I wished, instead of the commander of thousands of men in a carefully planned operation, with all the responsibilities attached. Then I shook off these thoughts and kept an eye on the ground below, which I knew pretty well by now, in case we had to force-land.

As I gazed out into the night I did a quick check in my mind. We were just over an hour behind schedule, which wasn't bad considering the sudden change in plan. It had meant a lot of extra work and reloading of gliders; I was afraid this had not been done with the care that is essential in air loading, but the men had done their best in the time available. Looking ahead, we had several nights of good moon for the build-up and if all went well I was determined to get cracking with our offensive tasks as soon as possible. The Japs would soon know where we were and the quicker we could act the more advantage we would get from our sudden and, I hoped, unexpected appearance in their midst.

We were flying in to approach our objective from the south and suddenly I saw the railway below us around the area where Bernard Fergusson and I had been blowing holes in it a year before. This time Bernard, with his 16 Brigade, had marched into Burma again, much further north. I envied him his footslogging at that moment, for I was beginning to hate the swaying movement of the glider and longed to be down on the ground.

Now I could see the Irrawaddy below, near Katha, and we swung north to approach the mouth of the Kaukkwe, a tributary of the big river. Broadway was in the Kaukkwe valley and the river itself ran along close to one side of the stronghold. I woke the others and told them we were approaching the target. Opposite me Lance-Corporal Young, my Anglo-Chinese batman, eased the tension by cracking a few jokes in his usual cheerful way. Suddenly, below, I spotted Broadway and then we cut the tow. The Dakota's engines faded away and a tremendous silence enveloped us, weird and frightening after the sound of the familiar and comforting machinery that had carried us through the air. Now it had gone and whatever happened we could not turn back.

I kept my eye at my peephole, with an occasional glance at Lees, who sat relaxed as if driving a Cadillac on a wide American motorway. His jaws kept moving rhythmically. We banked steeply and the ground came up in a rush. There was a hefty bump and I thought we were down, but almost at once we took off again, nose in the air. I looked forward, startled. Lees was still chewing gum, a fraction quicker now. Crash! A stanchion of the glider thumped me in the small of the back. Miraculously we were down, and still alive.

'All out,' I shouted, and helped free a sergeant whose hand had been crushed by one of the glider's stanchions, before I jumped to the ground myself to get my bearings. I set up my headquarters at the place I had already picked out from the aerial photograph, then made a quick tour of the landing area. The glider in front of ours had had its undercarriage wrenched off in a ditch and I saw why we had bumped and taken off again. Lees had spotted the wreck on the ground and with amazing split-second skill and presence of mind had managed to take our glider leapfrogging over it. There were two of these ditches running across the landing area; in fact they were drag paths along which elephants hauled timber to the river during the monsoon. They had not shown up in the aerial photographs and they were responsible for much of the chaos and several lives that night.

John Allisson and his men were already putting out the flares which were to guide in the next group of gliders and Lieutenant-Colonel Scott, commanding the 1st King's (Liverpool) Regiment, was on patrol with his men to make sure no Japs were around. All six of the advance-party gliders had landed and the plan had been that we would wheel them off to make way for the next batch, which would in turn be wheeled away and so on. But we had reckoned without the ditches. Three of the six gliders were so badly wrecked that the small force at present on the ground could not shift them. We worked at them furiously but suddenly I heard a shout and looked up. In the bright light of the moon I saw to my horror that the first two of the next batch had cast off and were winging their silent way down.

The first few landed safely, avoiding the obstacles on the ground, which included a couple of lone trees in the centre of the runway. But several of this batch were also wrecked by the ditches and became immovable in their turn, adding to the hazards for those still to come. More gliders sailed down to increase the chaos on the ground, crashing into the wreckage as they landed. All those that we could move we hauled away to the sides but we were constantly dashing into cover, all but run down by the following batches. To make matters worse, some of the pilots were having trouble judging the correct height to come in and several gliders crashed into the trees surrounding the runway. At times the rending, tearing, crunching sound of wings and fuselages being torn apart was quite deafening, then all would be quiet for a moment until the cries of the wounded men arose up from the wrecks.

Their pitiful calls for help pierced into my shocked mind as I worked with the others to clear up the mess. I was in command here. How much of this chaos and suffering was due to lack of foresight on my part? How much British blood was on my hands tonight? Surely we could have spotted somehow that those cursed ditches were running across the runway? If they hadn't been there . . . Furiously I shook myself to clear away these thoughts. In situations like this the first duty of a C.O. is to keep his head; later, perhaps, he can indulge in an orgy of self-condemnation, but not while he is still in action. He must plan to make the best of a bad job, rally the men he has left and lead them on in the hope that he can make up in some small way for the lives lost.

A warning shout broke into my thoughts. 'Look out, sir!' I swung round and saw a glider coming down almost straight at me. I dived out of its path and watched fascinated as it hit the ground clear of any wrecks but too near the edge of the runway to stop in safety. There was a tremendous crash as the wings were taken off by two trees, leaving the fuselage to hurtle on into the bush like a charging elephant. I felt certain there could be no survivors.

At last, thank God, the procession of gliders came to an end. The first wave had landed at Broadway. And the picture was a grim one. John Allisson had done a wonderful job in appalling circumstances and Colonel Scott and his men had worked valiantly setting up a dressing station, collecting the wounded and hauling gliders and wreckage away. I tried to weigh up the situation. It was too early yet to know the full extent of the damage and casualties here on the ground, but I feared they would be heavy. I also knew that many of the first wave of gliders had not turned up at Broadway at all and must have crashed on the way or gone off course. Before leaving Lalaghat I had arranged a code with Wingate. If things went well I would signal 'Pork Sausage', the favourite dish in the cook-house; if they went badly I would send 'Soya Link', the sausage meat substitute we all loathed. Surveying the scene around me at about four o'clock on the morning of March 6th I knew which words I would have to send; but, like anyone else, I hate having to admit failure. Finally, and very reluctantly, I ordered 'Soya Link' to go out.

Having made this unpalatable decision I suddenly felt completely exhausted and flopped down to the ground at my H.Q. while somebody gave me some cocoa. Allisson joined me and we discussed the situation for a few minutes before dozing off where we were. Some sleep was essential if I was to keep my mind fresh and active; but an hour or so later we were woken with a cry of 'Gliders' and two latecomers swished down and landed safely in the grey light of dawn, after losing their way and wandering around behind their Dakota until they found us. Soon afterwards a smart figure of a man, wearing a monocle, marched up in correct style with thirty men all in step behind him. They came to a neat halt. 'Major Shuttleworth and thirty men of the 1st Battalion, the Lancashire Fusiliers, reporting for orders, sir.' What a welcome sight and sound that was, a real slice of military order and discipline after a night of confusion and disaster.

After I had sent the major off to his post I was startled to hear the roar of a powerful engine coming, as far as I could tell, from the jungle, near the spot where the glider that had nearly hit me had vanished. Allisson joined me and we stared in amazement as a bulldozer slowly emerged from between the trees with a U.S. Army engineer, Lieutenant Brocket, at the controls. If I had had Aladdin's lamp with me that morning I would have told the genie to get me another bulldozer; one had landed safely but we badly needed a second to help clear the runway and, perhaps, save the whole situation.

Brocket rumbled up and told us his story. Because of the bulldozer's weight only two men could fly with it. So the big machine had been clamped down in one of the Waco gliders and Brocket had sat next to the pilot in the co-pilot's seat, with no other passengers. As they came down to Broadway they could see little room amid the wreckage, so the pilot had landed in such a way that the wings would be knocked off by trees but the fuselage would run clear. By good luck or good judgement, probably a mixture of both, this plan worked. On a Waco glider the pilot's and co-pilot's seats are attached to the part of the nose which opens upwards for unloading, and as they crashed into the Jungle Brocket and his pilot found themselves swung into the air in their seats. At the same time the bulldozer broke loose with the force of the impact and shot forward under them into the bush. The nose then swung down again and they returned to their place in a partly wrecked and completely empty glider. After recovering from this shock they clambered out, retrieved the bulldozer, got it going and came out now to report for duty.

The calm correctness of the monocled major and the resourcefulness of the young American engineer cheered and encouraged me. At one stage all had seemed hopeless but, as so often happens, the situation had appeared to be worse than it really was. It was possible now in the early dawn to work out our losses and our assets. I called in my senior officers and we set about the task.

Our casualties amounted to about thirty killed and the same number injured. But more than 350 officers and men had landed unharmed. In all, sixty-two gliders had taken off from Lalaghat. Of these thirty-five landed at Broadway, eight were recalled when I sent 'Soya Link', eight crash-landed on the Allied side of the India-Burma border and the rest made forced landings in Japanese-occupied parts of Burma. About half of the officers and men in the gliders which failed to reach Broadway managed to make their way back to base in Assam and joined us later. The remaining sixty-six men did not return.

We found later that the crashed gliders, scattered in various parts of northern Burma between the Irrawaddy and Assam, threw the Japs into complete confusion. They could see no reason for the crazy British to land troops in such widely dispersed and utterly unsuitable places. On the other hand it could just conceivably be part of some devilishly clever plan. In other words, the haphazard and unintentional landings proved an excellent piece of deception and it was some time before the Japanese discovered Broadway and the strength of the Chindit forces in their midst.

Of course, much of this was unknown to us at the time, but even so I began to feel more cheerful as we surveyed the situation at Broadway. Young Brocket reported that, apart from his bulldozers, one of his jeeps had landed safely with a scraper, which would be of great assistance with the clearing job ahead. Only seven of his engineers had survived the landing, but he assured Allisson and myself that if we allowed him some of Scott's men he could have a Dakota landing strip ready by evening. I rather doubted it but I was prepared to let him have a go and reckoned that, in any case, he could clear enough to get some light planes in to fly out the injured.

On the strength of this I sent a second signal, 'Pork Sausage', two or three hours after I had sent 'Soya Link'. It was received with joy at Lalaghat and later I spoke by wireless to Wingate. He had had his first taste that night of the horrors of high command: sitting at a table listening to reports of gliders crashing and going astray, and realizing that although his plans were not working as he had hoped he could do nothing about it. Always, before, he had gone out with his men, sharing the risks and the dangers and being on the spot to change his ideas to meet new emergencies. Now he could only sit, watch, wait and pray. It must have been a harrowing experience for a man like Orde. Slim, who had been through it all before, sat with him and I was told later that the Field Marshal had been a tower of strength all through, remaining absolutely calm. Just having him there with them, quiet and sensible, was a tremendous help to Wingate and his staff in their nerve-stretching ordeal.

I did not improve the situation by sending 'Soya Link', for at Lalaghat they assumed it meant we had been attacked by the Japs. But it had the desired effect of stopping any further flights that night. I hate to think what would have happened if any more gliders had tried to land on top of the mess on our runway.

During the day this wreckage gradually disappeared as Brocket and his men toiled in the heat and the dust almost without a break. A dozen small planes came in as soon as there was enough space for them and, much to my relief, flew the injured men back to Assam. For the gallant pilots it meant 400 miles of daylight flying over enemy-held territory in unarmed light aircraft. By skimming the trees and setting a careful course across the wild country beneath them they succeeded without loss and went on to fly many a dangerous sortie over the next few months to keep up our vital air life-line with India.

While all this was going on I went out to look for a site for the main stronghold area and soon found what I wanted, an excellent position which dominated not only the runway but also the whole surrounding area. Back at the clearing Lieutenant Brocket was proving me wrong and soon it was clear that he would have his Dakota strip ready as promised, complete with landing lights.

Sixty-five American and R.A.F. Daks came in that night bringing 900 more men plus stores and mules. Wingate flew in to see for himself what we were doing and we discussed the setting-up of the stronghold area and our future plans for attack before he went back to Lalaghat. Next morning work began on the stronghold defences and I selected sites for the field and anti-aircraft artillery which was coming in on the next flight. And still there was no sign of the enemy, thanks mainly to our complete air supremacy which kept their reconnaissance flights in check.

On the air strip the final touches were completed. My senior

R.A.F. officer, Squadron Leader Bobbie Thompson, who was part of my Brigade H.Q. staff and carried out the vital task of air liaison, reported back to base: 'La Guardia has nothing on us. Can take 100 a night.' And for the next few nights we did take an average of 100 Daks. At the same time 111 Brigade was flown in, partly to Chowringhee and partly to Broadway. By March 13th the build-up of both brigades, plus support troops, was complete, which meant that in seven nights about 9,000 men, 1,350 animals, 250 tons of stores, and batteries of field and anti-aircraft guns had landed in the heart of Burma, behind the enemy lines. To the north, another 3,000 men had marched in under Fergusson.[1]

Wingate issued an Order of the Day which contained his much-quoted phrase: 'All our columns are inside the enemy's guts.' Some people have used this to sneer at his flamboyant language and showman-like attitude. In fact it was an accurate description of the situation couched in unambiguous language that any soldier could understand. Thanks to the Air Force boys we were, indeed, inside the enemy's guts and it was now up to us to start giving him a stomach-ache.

[1] 16th Infantry Brigade comprising 45th Reconnaissance Regiment, 2nd Bn Leicestershire Regiment, 2nd Bn Queens Royal Regiment (West Surrey) and the 51st/69th Field Regiment, Royal Artillery as infantry.

19

Steel against Steel

The first real battle of the second Chindit campaign was a hand-to-hand affair which we started with a bayonet charge against a group of Japanese who were trying to stop us setting up a block on the railway line. It turned out to be the most vicious and bloody fight I have ever been in. An official account issued afterwards by Special Force headquarters said that 'it was at times, almost medieval' in its savagery.

The main object of our campaign in 1944 had been laid down at the Quebec Conference: to help General 'Vinegar Joe' Stilwell and his Chinese armies in their offensive from Yunnan against the Japs in northern Burma. This was the attack that had been put off in 1943 just before the first Chindit penetration. But now Stilwell and his American staff had a powerful force of Chiang Kai-shek's men facing the Japs and they were relying on us to cut the enemy's lines of communication running up from the south. The railway, which the Japs had got back into use after our demolition raids the year before, was one of these lines and a vital link for the enemy's famous 18th Division.

I was anxious to switch over to our offensive role as soon as possible but first we had to consolidate our position. One of the essentials of any attacking operation is a strong, firm base from which to work and that is what Broadway became in the week or two after our landing. We set up a hospital where the wounded could be treated while waiting to be flown back to India. We opened shops to barter goods with Burmese villagers from the surrounding area, and to pick up gossip which might be useful for intelligence purposes. We started a chicken farm, then went a step further and planted crops. Our airstrip in the heart of enemy-held Burma became so efficient that for a time a Spitfire wing was based there, and it remained our light plane base until the monsoon.

We also set deep and strong defences; but I have always agreed with the saying that attack is the best form of defence, so we wasted little time in getting after the enemy. I sent Major David Monteith, with his Lancashire Fusiliers, south to the Irrawaddy, where they stopped all traffic on the river which might have helped the Japs. Colonel Scott and the two columns of his battalion roamed the countryside around Broadway, watching for any enemy concentrations, giving Monteith a hand when necessary and generally keeping an eye on things.

I was impatient myself to get into action and at last the time came to move out against the railway, where I planned to set up another block or stronghold straddling the line. I left Claud Rome behind in charge of Broadway and took five columns with me on a march south-west towards the railway town of Mawlu. It felt good to be marching again and I was only too glad to leave the administrative worries of Broadway to Claud, who was a wonderful second-in-command and never complained at being handed the rough end to hold by his much younger C.O.

The jungle varies in Burma from the dark, dank primeval stuff with enormous creepers to sylvan glades with rippling streams and even, in a few places, tall, straight trees with little or no undergrowth at all, like a pine forest. In the Kaukkwe valley, which we had to cross, it was the dank type and slowed up some of the columns. One column in particular, under Major Shuttleworth, got into a really dense area; it was so bad that when he was asked what supplies he wanted in the next air drop Shuttleworth radioed hopefully for a path! Because of the greater jungle experience of Brigade H.Q. we got along faster and were the first to reach the hilltop overlooking the railway near Mawlu; I had, in fact, intended to get there first so that I could take a good look round and change my plan if necessary. I discovered that Mawlu had a Japanese garrison of about 500 men, so I decided to establish the block on the line about a mile and a half to the north, at a place called Henu.

I sent a Gurkha column to put in a diversionary attack to the north at Nansiang, then return to me in reserve, while three other columns set out to establish the block. Shuttleworth's column was already operating to the south of us. All seemed to go well. The Gurkhas, under Freddie

Shaw, came back from Nansiang and we were discussing their action there when I heard firing from the direction of the block. We set out at once to find out what was going on.

The site of the block was a group of small hills thirty to fifty feet high, with lots of little valleys running between them, beside the railway at Henu. As we got nearer the sound of firing increased and it seemed that quite a scrap was going on. I called up one of the column commanders, Ron Degg, on a walkie-talkie, and he guided us along a ridge to the spot where a group of Japs had infiltrated between his column and one of the others. Suddenly we saw a crowd of Jap soldiers milling round a pagoda on top of a little hill overlooking the flat paddy land through which the railway ran. The Japs had not seen us so we got down quietly and shot them up before they realized we were there.

The enemy quickly took cover and then I noticed some of Degg's South Staffords in an exposed position across the valley. They were in trouble and needed help quickly. I told Freddie Shaw to give me covering fire while I went across to them with Bobbie Thompson and my two loyal and ever-present shadows, my batman, Lance-Corporal Young, and my groom, Paddy Dermody. We got across safely, actually passing behind a group of Japs who were a little mixed up by now and so unsure about where they were supposed to be firing that they were looking the wrong way.

I saw a number of dead and wounded as I scrambled up the hill to where Degg's men were crouching. 'Thank God you've come, sir,' one of them said; they had had a bad time. They told me that the Japs had surprised them and attacked soon after they had reached the site, before they were properly dug in. As far as they knew the enemy force, which had clearly moved in from Mawlu just up the line had come at them first from the direction of Henu village and were now centred on Pagoda Hill.

Surprise had been on the Japs' side this time and it seemed to me that shock tactics were needed if we were to succeed in ejecting them from the Henu area and setting up our block. If we could get them off that hill we would probably win the day, but if we allowed them to stay there and consolidate their position it would take God knows what to shift them and might easily wreck the whole operation. From there they could dominate the area and stop us reaching the railway line, and I was determined they should not do that. As for the South

Staffords, they were looking rather shattered. For some of them — reinforcements after Tobruk — it was their first taste of battle and the horror and fear that go with it as friends you were talking to a moment before fall dead, or screaming from a dreadful wound. But they were good, stout men, well trained and well led; I decided that they also needed a shock, to jerk them back to life and action.

I looked back to the valley we had crossed and saw that Freddie Shaw was beginning to lead his Gurkhas over to join us. I yelled to him that we were going to charge and to follow us as soon as he had got his men across. Then I stood up and bellowed 'Charge', ignoring the amazed look on the faces of some of the Staffords, who clearly thought I was mad. With Bobbie, Young and Dermody I ran full tilt down the slope and into the valley which divided us from Pagoda Hill, praying the rest would follow. Halfway down I heard a commotion behind and, glancing round, saw about half the Staffords pounding down after us; but the rest had stayed put. 'What the hell d'you think you're doing?' I screamed, striving to be heard above the racket of the men who were now rushing past me. 'Charge, you bastards, charge!'

Looking back, I just don't know what I would have done if they had ignored me a second time. Luckily the situation didn't arise. I don't know whether it was my shouting or the sight of their friends and comrades rushing towards the enemy that moved them; whatever it was they moved, every one of them, machine-gunners, mortar teams, the lot. I saw that the Gurkhas, too, were getting ready to follow, so I turned and crossed the valley and started up Pagoda Hill.

A number of the first wave of Staffords were now in front of me, scrambling up the slope without a pause as if the whole thing had been their idea and they couldn't wait to get at the enemy's throat. I was close on their heels at the top and it now occurred to me that the Japs had been strangely quiet. Some shots had come down at us but not as many as I had expected, which probably meant we had regained the initiative by then and taken them unawares. Then, to my surprise, the Japs leapt up as we went at them and charged into us. Two sides charging at each other was certainly not going according to the military rule books.

We clashed in an area of about fifty square yards on the hilltop and the air was filled with the sound of steel crashing against steel, the screams and curses of wounded men, the sharp crack of revolver and

152

rifle shots, the eerie whine of stray bullets and the sickening crunch of breaking bones. Everybody slashed and bashed at the enemy with any weapon that came to hand, yelling and shouting as they did so. In Europe the cold steel part of it would have been restricted to bayonets; out here there was more variety, with the Japanese officers wielding their huge swords and the Gurkhas doing sterling work with the kukri, the curved knife they used with such deadly effect. The official report I quoted earlier summed it up: 'The characteristic of this fighting was its savagery . . . rifle and bayonet against two-handed feudal sword, kukri against bayonet, no quarter to the wounded . . .'

In front of me I saw a young Staffords subaltern, Lieutenant Cairns, attacked by a Japanese officer who viciously hacked off his arm with a sword. Cairns shot the Jap point-blank, flung away his revolver and picked up the sword that had maimed him before leading his men on, slashing fiercely at any Jap within his reach. Finally he dropped to the ground mortally wounded, but that gallant youngster refused to die until the battle was over. I was able to speak to him before he closed his eyes for the last time. 'Have we won, sir? Was it all right? Did we do our stuff? Don't worry about me.'

Is it any wonder that, so many years later, some of us still have nightmares? There is glory in a fight like this. But there is horror in it, too, as young lives are brought abruptly and brutally to an end and young bodies maimed and made useless. Later Cairns was awarded the Victoria Cross; but he never knew it.

At the time, of course, there is no room for such thoughts as these, no room for anything except the fight. I can still remember the faithful Young and Dermody battling at my side, Young shouting anxiously, 'Be careful, sir, be careful' as he shot at any Jap who came within his vision. Then, at last, we drove them back behind the pagoda and there was a brief intermission as both sides lobbed grenades over and around the battered house of worship; fortunately the Jap grenade has a lot of bark but not much bite, so they did little harm. But they added to the noise and confusion and I found it difficult to think out our next step amid the shambles of the battleground.

In the back of my mind I felt sure that one last heave would win us the day. Then someone came up and said we were short of ammunition. It occurred to me at once that if we were short the Japs, who had been in action longer, would be even shorter. That was one important point to our advantage. Then I noticed that the Japs were up to their usual trick of yelling at us in English: 'Give up, Tommy,' 'Why do you want to die?' and so on. There was a little more variety in some of the phrases and I thought it possible that at least one of them had a fair command of English. Perhaps this would give us that extra chance I had been searching for in my mind.

I turned my face towards the Japs so they could hear me clearly and shouted: 'We'll retreat as fast as possible in this direction.' I stuck out my arm and the men saw I was pointing towards the pagoda. 'Staffords to the right, Gurkhas left,' I yelled, and every man who was not wounded raced off round the pagoda and fell on the startled Japs once more. This was too much for the enemy. They broke and ran, hurling themselves down the other side of Pagoda Hill and across the paddy land at the bottom towards Henu village, and we went after them. It was wonderful to see the so-called invincible conquerors of the Pacific going at full stretch to get away from British guns and British steel. So much for the image of the 'unbeatable Jap' which had been built up in so many Allied minds since their tremendous victories of 1942. I saw a young Gurkha turn over a dead Jap with his foot and look amazed when he saw that the enemy soldier had certainly been no older than he was, and in fact looked fresh-faced and innocent in death. I could almost hear the Gurkha saying to himself: 'Are these the supermen we are meant to fear?'

The South Staffords and the Gurkhas shifted the enemy out of Henu later in the day and found their man-pack flame throwers a very useful weapon for clearing dug-outs without exposing themselves to traps. The remnants of the enemy force, which had come so near to wrecking our plans for a block on the railway, retreated rapidly towards Mawlu, and we took pot shots at them as they crossed the open paddy outside Henu.

By this time I had been told the extent of our casualties. Fourteen officers had taken part in the bayonet charge; three of these had been killed and four wounded. This fifty-per-cent figure gives an illustration of the part individual leadership plays in this type of close warfare. An officer must be in front of his men, leading them on by personal example. But the price is heavy. Most of those who survived on Pagoda Hill were killed later.

Among the other ranks we had twenty killed and sixty wounded that day, but it had not been in vain. We counted forty-two Japs dead on and around Pagoda Hill and others were killed or wounded as they tried to escape across the paddy. So, although ours had been a heavy loss, the Japanese had come off worse, and they had also been well and truly beaten. For our part, sad as we were about our casualties, we felt elated at our victory. It set a standard for the brigade, and gave everyone something to live up to. Victory for a unit in its first scrap is a great morale-builder and lays the seeds in the minds of all for further successes. Another good omen was that fortune had been on our side: firstly, direct air support from Cochrane's boys had kept the remaining Japs pinned down in Mawlu so that they could not come out to help their comrades; secondly, we discovered from documents that most of the enemy troops were engineers and, bravely as they had fought, they were not fully trained to infantry standards. We were lucky to have been blooded against second-class opposition.

The battle had taken place on March 18th and that night we had a big supply drop, including entrenching tools, wire and ammunition. During the next few nights the Japs made occasional probing attacks on our defences, which helped us to patch up the weak spots but otherwise had little effect. More supplies were dropped and the new stronghold became known as White City because of the shrouds of white parachutes draped over the trees all around us. A light plane strip was also prepared on the flat land between the railway line and Pagoda Hill and our wounded were evacuated to Broadway and on to India.

Wingate flew in to see us during the build-up and told me of some of his headaches back at headquarters; he would much rather have been in action with us. Part of the trouble was that, at the same time as our fly-in to Broadway, the Japanese had begun an advance from their positions along the Chindwin, with Imphal and Kohima as their objectives. At this new threat to India some of Wingate's critics got in a flap and began complaining that the Chindits had been flown too far into Burma to be of any use to 4th Corps, who were defending the Assam border; they conveniently ignored the fact that our declared object was to help Stilwell. This Japanese move towards Assam also brought out the worst of Vinegar Joe's well-known anti-British feelings. Wingate told me that Stilwell had

155

said he intended to slow up his advance towards Myitkyina in the north 'in case the Limeys ran away' in Assam and left him exposed to the full weight of the enemy forces in northern Burma. He was the sort of person who wore Allied friendship very thin at times.

I am a soldier, not a politician, and I was glad to be away from all this high-powered bickering (although I was to become involved in it later). As for Wingate, he seemed to be able to relax for an hour or two with us in White City, where the atmosphere of bustle and action and practicality must have seemed far removed from the thick air of theory, planning and petty squabbles at headquarters. He insisted on walking along the railway line which he had risked so much to capture. 'So this is 18 Division's rail communication,' he said, kicking the line as we walked. It was good to see him in that mood again.

Wingate's visit left us in good heart and just at that moment we needed all the encouragement we could get, for it was plain that trouble was brewing. The number of Jap pin-prick raids was increasing and it was pretty obvious they were part of the prelude to a big attack. It came on the night of March 21st and before it ended I had lost one of my closest helpers and friends.

Again it was the South Staffords who bore the brunt of the fighting and during the night the Japs got a foothold on two positions within the White City perimeter, albeit at great loss to themselves. Our 3-inch mortars broke up attacks on other defence sectors but intermittent fighting went on for most of the night. Towards dawn Colonel Richards of the South Staffords asked me for two platoons to launch a counter-attack on the Japs who had broken through. I sent him the men he wanted and at first light he led them himself in a whirlwind charge which drove the enemy from White City and restored our defence position. The colonel had shown outstanding courage but he was badly wounded in the chest.

I went forward to see what damage the Japs had done and, as always, Young and Paddy Dermody were with me. We had named one of our hills Bare Hill, because most of the trees on its slopes had been cut down, and as we went up it Paddy shouted 'Look out, sir,' and gave me a shove. At the same time he fell himself, badly wounded in the groin. I charged round a tree trunk and emptied my revolver into a wounded Jap who had fired at us, then Young and I carried Paddy down to the dressing station. Bare Hill was supposed to be clear of the enemy but I suspected more were there so I sent in the Gurkhas to clear it. They killed eleven Japs who had stayed behind either because they were wounded or because they wanted to take some of us with them before committing suicide. They could have caused a lot of trouble if we hadn't found them so quickly.

Back at the dressing station our two doctors were doing a magnificent job, working non-stop on the wounded and up to their elbows in blood. Our padres were helping to comfort the men and I spoke to some of them, including Richards and Paddy, who was in great pain.

It was sad for me to see him like that, for he was a great little man. He was a former jockey who had joined the Irish Free State Army and became a sergeant. In 1940 he decided the British needed a bit of strengthening from the Irish and marched his whole platoon on to the boat for Liverpool, where they all volunteered for the King's (Liverpool) Regiment.

When the King's joined the Chindits Wingate took Paddy as his groom and he came to me later. He taught me a lot about riding. I sat in the saddle with my toes out, military style. 'Never ride like that, sir,' he said, 'it's so easy for another rider to tip you off.' He came up alongside me, put his foot under mine and the next moment I was on the ground. 'You see what I mean, sir,' Paddy said with rather more than his usual touch of brogue, for I was a brigadier and he was an acting corporal. He helped me up. 'I could never have done that if you kept your toes down.'

My pony Jean and several others had been flown in with the mules and in some parts of the jungle – not the really dense stuff – I would move around from unit to unit by pony. We always carried four-second grenades and Paddy and I and a few others had perfected a method of throwing them while riding. We had hooks fixed on to our saddles so that we could get the pin out with one hand while keeping hold of the reins with the other.

We put this into practice one day when I was out with Paddy and several others, about six in all, in the area around White City. We came upon a party of Japs quite suddenly. They far outnumbered us and it was a moment for swift decision. We spurred on our ponies and raced past the enemy patrol, hurling grenades as fast as we could before they had a chance to stop us. We went flat out and never looked back, in case more Japs were around, but we must have done quite a lot of damage and it was pleasing to know that the time we had spent working on this exercise had now paid off. It must have been the last cavalry charge of the British Army!

The fierce fighting around White City went on for another day or so, but by the 23rd the Japs had retired, beaten, to Mawlu. Once again close air support had helped us enormously; once again our casualties were high. We had thirty-four killed, including six officers, and forty-two wounded. Our consolation was that we had inflicted at least twice as many casualties on the Japs.

We continued our defence build-up and a day or two later Wingate flew in again. He visited every part of the block and chatted to everyone he saw, making useful suggestions and generally cheering us up. He showed me messages of congratulation on the opening phase of the second Chindit operation from Churchill and Roosevelt, and was obviously pleased with them. But his general attitude to this sort of thing was that awards and pats on the back should not be allowed to breed over-confidence, which might affect one's judgement.

I had been awarded a D.S.O. for the first Chindit campaign and before he left White City Wingate said: 'Oh, by the way, you have a bar to your D.S.O.' This was for the fly-in to Broadway and the battle at Pagoda Hill. He added: 'Let it go to your heart and not to your head.'

After that we waved him off in his light plane and never saw him again.

He flew first to visit Fergusson at the stronghold site he had just chosen, about sixteen miles north-west of White City, which became known as Aberdeen. From there Wingate went back to Broadway, changed from his light plane into the Mitchell bomber that had brought him into Burma that morning, and flew back to Imphal. Later that day he took off again to visit Cochrane at Lalaghat, and several other people, two British war correspondents among them, were also in the Mitchell. They all died instantly when it came down on a mountain slope and burst into flames which helped to wipe out any chance of finding a clue to the reason for the crash.[1]

---

[1] A full account can be found in the book 'The Death of Wingate' by Dennis Hawley, Merlin Books ISBN number 0–86303–677–5. Obtainable from the author at Yew Tree Cottage, Yew Tree Lane, Slaithwaite, Huddersfield HD7 5UD.

More than a week passed before we heard the news. It had been delayed while a party from Chindit rear headquarters in Assam trekked out to make positive identification. Then Wingate's wife Lorna had to be informed before any announcement could be made.

It is difficult to express in words the horror and dismay we felt. The Chindits were Wingate's dream, which he had made come true in the face of tremendous opposition. Even the men in Special Force who had seen him only once or twice at a distance felt the shock of his loss as it reverberated down the lines of command. The Chindits would fight on, but they would never be quite the same again without the man who created and inspired them.

20

The Headhunters

Every commander must be something of an actor. Showmanship is one of the basic arts of leadership, in both military and civilian life. Churchill with his cigar and his V-sign; Montgomery with his Tank Corps beret and 'hit 'em for six' pep talks. Without these tricks of the trade they would not have made the necessary impact on the people who were looking up to them to set an example. Whatever their real feelings were, they had to appear cheerful and confident in public.

This same principle applied right down the line and it was brought home to me in a frightening way during one of the Japanese attacks on White City. I was with a mobile column exploring the area outside the perimeter and the enemy, who had thrown a large force against the block, had pinned us down in a difficult position with three machine-guns firing away almost continuously. Luckily they were aiming high, a few feet above our heads as we lay flattened on the ground, but it was an unnerving experience and we were in a tough spot. I reckoned that mortar shells might shift the Japs but at the moment our mortars were all busy elsewhere. Something had to be done so I decided to make a dash for the nearest mortar away to our right.

I set out at a run for the mortar site and found to my horror that several of the men began running as well. Maybe they thought I was getting out to save my skin and decided to join me. Or they might have been blindly following my lead, without thinking; it is not easy to think under enemy machine-gun fire. Whatever their reasoning they had to be stopped. I turned and yelled at them to get back to their positions. This brought them up short and they suddenly realized what they were doing. I shouted again and was relieved to see them dive back to their places. Then I turned and started walking towards the mortar; it was the only thing I could do. At every step I wanted desperately to break into a run again. But just as it was essential for Churchill to smile and make his V-sign, however downcast he felt himself, so it was essential for me, in front of my troops, to stroll through those Japanese bullets. I was acting then and it was the most hair-raising part I had ever played. Luckily for me, the Japanese supporting cast were either rotten shots or else they just didn't see me. I reached the mortar safely.

After the failure of the first Japanese attacks on White City I decided to put in an immediate counter-attack and we cleared the remaining Japs out of Mawlu. For the next week or ten days the enemy were licking their wounds and during this period we blew several bridges on the railway in the area and mined the roads. A Dakota strip was prepared and we improved our defences with more wire and mines and finally light artillery flown in from Broadway.

Meanwhile I practised some more showmanship, this time aimed at the Burmese. I rode around visiting the neighbouring villages on my white pony, complete with a mounted bodyguard under the command of my new groom, Ginger, who had taken Paddy's place. On these occasions I would get out my brigadier's red hat and felt like a true nineteenth-century pukkah sahib as the villagers bowed low at our arrival. I even distributed largesse; at Mawlu I gave the headman 1,500 rupees in payment for the damage we had done to Burmese property. The aim of all this parading about and showing the flag was to give an impression of calmness and complete superiority over the Japanese, so that the locals would be convinced we were the ones to back and pass on their information to us. But in this effort I was just a showpiece. The real job of intelligence and propaganda was done by my Burma Rifles company under Taffy Griffiths, their superb commanding officer who had been in the country for years in forestry.

It was during this time that we heard of Wingate's death and the subsequent appointment of Brigadier William 'Joe' Lentaigne to succeed him with the rank of Major-General. Joe was in command of 111 Brigade – now operating with great success against Jap road transport and supply dumps to the west of us – but he had never been in Wingate's confidence to the extent that one or two others had been, including Brigadier Tulloch, Wingate's Chief of Staff, and myself. He was, however, a highly experienced commander and it was his experience and his stability that decided Slim in his favour. The task of following in Wingate's footsteps was an unenviable one. The men who had opposed Orde's ideas but who had been unable to shift him because of his powerful friends now had a new and comparatively unprotected target. The knives that had been reluctantly put away were taken out again and lovingly sharpened.

A week or so after Joe took over he held a conference of brigade commanders at Aberdeen to take stock of our position and plan our future operations. It was a memorable meeting, with Bernard Fergusson a flawless host, and it reached a successful conclusion as far as I was concerned, for it was agreed that I should get on the move again. White City would be taken over by our West African brigade while I set out north to try to link up with Stilwell's forces.

Soon after my return to White City the Africans began to arrive and I made my plans for moving out. But it is dangerous to hope for too much in war, particularly the sort of war we were fighting. Reports of increasing Japanese activity began coming in. They took over Mawlu again and it soon became clear that they were now concentrating fresh troops around us for a second and more determined attack on the block. They were in strength this time, supported by artillery, and their bombardment opened up on the night of April 6th.

Our twenty-five-pounders, not yet fully dug in, answered some of the enemy fire, which lasted about an hour. Then came the first attack, with the usual wild yells and shouts as the Japs charged at our defences. We lit up the perimeter with mortar star-shells then mowed down the unfortunate little yellow men with machine-gun and rifle fire and grenades. They had soon had enough and retired, but a few hours later another bombardment started up, followed by the second attack. Again we beat them off and when dawn came our casualties were only two killed and six injured. For the Japs it was a different story. We found many of them dead and dying on our wire and a number had been killed trying to burst through with Bangalore torpedoes. These are normally carried by three suicide men, stripped of most of their clothing, who throw themselves and the torpedo at the wire to try to blast a hole through. The fact that they failed says much for our defences.

That was the first of many attacks the Japs flung at White City during the next ten days. The pressure and strain on everyone there was tremendous. The bombardments became more intense each day and the Japs got more and more on target. We were cooped up in our stronghold and had to sit there and take it; I can remember lying in my dug-out and giving way to uncontrollable fits of shivering, brought on partly through fear and partly through frustration. A running fight, a bold action on the move with a chance to hit back – they are easier on the mind and on the nerves. A bombardment is soul-destroying.

The strain took different people different ways. I tried to get out to visit the men on the perimeter as often as possible and one night I went up to the Lancashire Fusiliers sector, where a lot of shouting was going on. I found that a sergeant and his men, surrounded by grenades, were playing a sort of 'peek-a-boo' game with the enemy troops opposite. An English-speaking Jap would shout: 'You dirty British bastards,' and the fusiliers would fling a cluster of grenades in the direction of the voice. Then the Lancashire sergeant would roar out: 'You bloody yellow bastards,' and back would come a shower of grenades from the enemy. The throwing was pretty wild but it didn't seem to matter. At least the fusiliers were getting rid of some of their frustration and for a short while I joined in their game of death-or-miss. It was, as the psychiatrists say, an outlet.

The Nigerians who had just flown in were manning another part of the perimeter with great gusto. Some of their methods were unorthodox, to put it mildly, but they were wonderful fighters and they were fresh and eager for battle. They took over one of our key defence points, O.P. Hill. Almost immediately the Japs attacked it fiercely and at one stage broke through the wire and established a forward post inside our line. But the Nigerians fought like fury. One of them suddenly saw a Jap face peering at him over the parapet of his trench, seized a box full of grenades by its rope handle and flattened the Jap's head with it. When dawn came the Nigerians counter-attacked with a bayonet charge. But this particular chap left his rifle and bayonet behind and just took his box. When he had chucked all the grenades at the Japs he started laying about him with the heavy container, breaking heads and generally enjoying himself. Unorthodox, as I said, but effective.

The Nigerians not only cleared the enemy off O.P. Hill, they also chased them some distance away over the paddy. Many of them did deadly work with their razor-sharp machetes, as I found when I visited their dug-outs soon afterwards. I told their British officer I would like to have a look round and he said quickly: 'I shouldn't do that, sir.' I didn't accept his advice but down in the dug-outs I saw what he meant. In each one a little niche had been carved in the wall, and carefully stacked inside were Jap heads the Nigerians had brought back as souvenirs of their victory.

We repaired the damage to our defences and the next night the Japs attacked again, but once more we beat them off and inflicted heavy casualties. The drain on our ammunition stocks was tremendous and I was furious to get a message from India saying they estimated that our food must be running low so they were sending more in, instead of ammunition. I sent back a signal: 'We can live without food but not without ammunition. Please send ammunition.' In fact men do not eat much during periods of continuous action and strain; we were not getting through our full rations. It is afterwards, when the reaction sets in, that food is essential. Rations should then be increased.

Despite five more days and nights of attack the West African Brigade continued to arrive by air in the occasional lulls. On April 11th Joe Lentaigne ordered me to form a counter-attack force outside the block to hit the Japs from behind as they flung themselves at White City. In view of the plan made at our Aberdeen conference I had already sent the first part of my strike force out of the block; I now arranged that the rest of us should join them at a rendezvous area a few miles west of White City. I sent off my Tactical Brigade H.Q. under my Brigade Major, Francis Stuart, and handed over the block to Brigadier Gillmore, commander of the West African Brigade. Then I flew out in a light plane to reconnoitre the area for my future operations.

I was never more thankful to get into an active role again. White City had become an altogether unpleasant place to live in by then. Apart from the pounding bombardments and the mental frustration of endless defence, the physical discomforts were mounting. The smell of death was everywhere. Our own dead we had buried in an area consecrated by the padres, and we also did the best we could to dispose of the mules and bullocks killed in the block. But on the wire around us were scores of Japanese bodies in various stages of decomposition and we could do little about them without endangering our own lives. The sun beat down and the stench was sickening. My light plane pilot told me: 'We can find White City easily now. We navigate by smell.' And he was not exaggerating.

21

A Toast to Death

Opinions differ on beards. Some people would not be without one while others can't stand them at any price. I can take them or leave them. I grew a big, black bushy one on the first Chindit campaign; this time I stayed clean-shaven. But in wartime beards definitely have their uses. If a man thinks he looks tough he will often be tough and, more important, act tough. Odd as it may seem I am sure that some of our chaps who came through safely would not have stayed the course without their beards.

I was therefore pleased to include in my strike force about 450 men of the Reconnaissance Regiment sent down to me from 16 Brigade at Aberdeen. These chaps were mostly Devonshires and many of them had grown great patriarchal beards during their long march into Burma under Fergusson. And they certainly proved their toughness in the next week or two. I also had the 7th Nigerian Rifles with me as well as my own 3/6 Gurkhas, the Lancashire Fusiliers and various headquarters units. In all we were about 2,400 strong.

We now knew that a place called Sepein, near Mawlu, was the central headquarters for the enemy forces attacking White City and I decided that this should be my main objective. We made our base at Thayaung, south of Mawlu, which I had chosen during my reconnaissance by air; there was good cover in the dry beds of a number of small streams and a clearing nearby which could quickly be made into a light plane strip for evacuating wounded. At dusk, as we set off from Thayaung, we heard the familiar thump-thump as the nightly Japanese bombardment of White City started up a few miles away. I reckoned that the block could not hope to hold out unless we could get the Japs on the run within the next few days. Time was therefore precious and I hoped that my calculated gamble of attacking Sepein without adequate reconnaissance patrolling would pay off.

At first all seemed well. Reports came back to Brigade H.Q. that the 3/6 Gurkhas had taken Sepein village and on the strength of that I sent off my reserve column of Nigerians, under Lieutenant-Colonel Peter Vaughan, to attack Mawlu. He took the Japs there by surprise and killed many of them in the outskirts of the village before going on to capture the railway station. Vaughan was so much in command of the area that he was able to evacuate his wounded along the railway line into White City. But by now the news from Sepein was worsening. I went off to see what was happening there, riding Jean flat out, and found that the main Japanese position was just beyond the village. They were well dug in and surrounded by thick scrub, which gave them excellent cover and made the attackers' task almost impossible. I wirelessed to the block for the twenty-five-pounders to help and they pumped 100 shells into the area. I also called on air support, and Cochrane's Mustangs bombed the Jap defences. But still we could not shift them. By then the men were exhausted and I decided to withdraw to Thayaung.

The gamble had not paid off. All would have been well if the enemy really had been in Sepein; but the momentum of our advance had been lost by the time we reached their real strongpoint outside the village. The ground reconnaissance I had decided to do without through lack of time would have shown us the true position and it depressed me to think that we might have gained our objective if it had not been for my impatience. Looking back, however, I don't see what else I could have done. My orders were to act quickly to relieve the block; and in fact we had achieved a certain amount by pulling some of the enemy away from the immediate White City area. Also, in the attacks on Sepein and Mawlu we had counted fifty enemy dead while our own casualties were sixteen killed and thirty-five wounded. So our efforts had been by no means in vain.

I now decided that our best move would be to cut the enemy's communications in the Mawlu-Sepein area and squeeze him between us and White City, so that he would have to fight at his front and rear at the same time. First, however, I wanted to rest my men, if only for a day or so. But it was not to be. I received an urgent signal from Brigadier Gillmore saying that unless the enemy could be shifted soon he could not guarantee to hold White City. There was nothing for it after that but to move off again as soon as the wounded had been flown out and we had replenished our supplies from an air drop.

We advanced with the Reconnaissance Regiment forming the spearhead immediately followed by my special 'élite' company of Gurkhas, under young Ian MacPherson, who acted as mobile reserve to go in whenever trouble was brewing. We went further north this time then turned in towards White City. We met odd pockets of Japs on the way but they were no match for our force and we killed thirty or forty that day without loss to ourselves. By dusk we had reached a point about a mile south-east of the block, an ideal spot from which to go for the enemy as they gathered to attack White City. We camped for the night but lit no fires and the Japs did not know we were there until the Reconnaissance Regiment took an enemy unit completely by surprise in a dawn raid. The reconnaissance boys drove a deep wedge into the Jap positions outside the block and the rest of the column moved up in support.

The battle was now well and truly on. The enemy realized that they were being attacked from the rear and turned on us ferociously. We estimated that well over 2,000 Japs were now squeezed between us and the block, which was only half a mile away at several points along our front. I had previously arranged with Gillmore that as we pushed the Japs against his defences he would launch an attack from the block itself, and during the morning we could hear the Nigerians from White City, as they broke out among the now bewildered enemy. But these Japs were good soldiers, well led and well equipped and willing to fight to the last man. They recovered and made a sudden counter-attack, catching my Brigade H.Q. in the crossfire of heavy machine-guns. We kept ourselves flat on the ground as the bullets scythed through the thick jungle undergrowth a couple of feet above our heads. The unfortunate mules carrying our wireless sets could not get down far enough. I watched fascinated as bullet holes appeared in rows along their bodies, little spurts of blood in line, before they crashed to the ground.

Suddenly we heard the roar of planes above our heads and I sighed with relief. Before the battle had really got going I had ordered the Mustangs for 1 p.m., when I reckoned the fighting would be at its height and they would be of most use. This time my gamble *had* paid off and my estimate was dead right. I rolled over and over until I was lying beside Mungo Park, my signals officer, who was in touch with White City on his wireless set. I asked the block signals people to tell the Mustangs they had to be absolutely accurate with their bombing and strafing, as we were very close to the Japs. To emphasize just how close we were Mungo told me I was shouting into the set and every time I spoke the Japs fired in the direction of my voice.

Then the Mustangs began diving, slap bang on target. We muffled our heads in our arms to shut out the roar of exploding bombs and the earth shivered and shook beneath our bellies. The strafing followed and again Cochrane's boys showed off their pin-point accuracy. The Jap machine-guns stopped abruptly and the intense feeling of relief at our release from that stuttering menace brought tears to my eyes.

We had all had enough and it was time to move. The question was, which way? As we discussed it the forward reconnaissance boys reported that several well-dug-in Jap machine-guns were still capable of firing along the narrow valley between us and the block where so many of our men had died already. So I decided to stay outside White City and return to Thayaung. We began to move off, and the weariness and exhaustion that is the aftermath of battle gradually took hold of us. I felt terrible, and it seemed to me that something was badly wrong. 'Where's Ian?' I asked suddenly, as I realized that it was his gay and carefree company that I was missing.

There was a pause and then Francis Stuart, my stalwart and utterly reliable brigade major, spoke quietly: 'He's dead.' It seemed impossible; surely nothing could kill Ian MacPherson.

'He can't be,' I said rather foolishly.

'I saw him shot through the forehead,' Francis replied.

I don't know what came over me then. All the tension and depression brought on by week after week of almost endless fighting and responsibility for men's lives, and deaths, seemed to overwhelm me. 'I don't believe it. I must go back and see for myself,' I said, and stopped in my tracks.

Francis looked at me, took out his revolver and stuck it in my stomach. 'I was with him when he was killed,' he said grimly. 'I'll shoot you if you turn back.'

The shock of what he said brought me to my senses. Behind us we could hear the rearguard engaging the remnants of the Japs. I would have to go through all that to find Ian's body. It was more than

169

likely I would be killed or captured, and to no purpose. My duty was to the brigade, not to just one man in it, even if that man was Ian MacPherson, one of the bravest soldiers I have ever met. Francis saw that I had recovered and put his pistol away. We walked on in silence, both knowing that he had done what he had to do.

We struggled slowly back and by midnight most of the men had reported in at Thayaung. The evacuation of the wounded started at dawn next day and by then we knew our casualties; between sixty and seventy British and Gurkha dead, 150 wounded and several missing. Our only consolation was that the Japs had lost even more. From White City we heard that the enemy dead were estimated at between 700 and 900. We also heard that the Japs were broken and had retreated from their offensive positions around White City; in fact they never attacked the block again. This news of success did little to lighten our hearts. We had lost too many good and brave men to feel like celebrating, and our minds and bodies were too tired. Information came in that the defeated Japs were slipping past us to safety, but we were in no state to go after them in strength. Individual raiding parties went out and caught some of the retreating enemy in ambush, but we would be useless as a combined fighting force until we got some rest.

With this in mind, and knowing that White City was no longer menaced, we moved off on April 25th and slowly made our way up into the coolness and comparative safety of the Kachin villages in the 3,000-foot hills of the Gangaw range, which ran more or less parallel with the railway. By this time the monsoon was nearly with us and it was decided by headquarters that the air strips at Broadway and White City would become unusable once the rains came. To many of us the thought of abandoning the two strongholds we had fought so hard to create and defend was almost unbearable. I was still very depressed and I also had an attack of malaria, and some of the messages I drafted to Joe Lentaigne were so insubordinate that the loyal Francis would not send them; it was just as well for me. As it was, the ones that did get through were pretty ripe. Joe was very good about it and probably appreciated how I was feeling, but in the end he had to give me a stiff warning, which I thoroughly deserved.

Finally Joe flew out to Broadway on May 8th, a few days before it was evacuated, to explain the position to the men on the spot. I went down from the hills to meet him and there he gave us a quick review of the Chindit situation. Of our original six brigades one, 23 Brigade, had been taken by 14th Army to help against the Japs in the Kohima area, leaving us with five. By this time 16 Brigade had been flown back to India from Aberdeen, which had then been abandoned; the bearded reconnaissance regiment had also gone out now. So there were four brigades left behind the Jap lines: my own, 77; the West Africans at White City; 14 Brigade, which had flown into Aberdeen – at about the same time as the West Africans joined us – and had since kept on the move attacking Jap transport and dumps whenever the chance arose; and 111 Lentaigne's old brigade now commanded by Jack (John) Masters, which had also played a mobile role.

Joe explained that all four brigades would now be moving north to get nearer to Stilwell and give him more direct support. In fact 111 Brigade had already made a rapid march and the day before had reached the area selected for a new stronghold, called Blackpool, on the railway line about fifty or sixty miles north of White City. The plan was for 14 Brigade to move up to help protect Blackpool from the west, and they would be joined by the West Africans after White City was evacuated in a couple of days' time. A few days later Claud Rome would evacuate Broadway and join up with me; then 77 Brigade, all together again, would move north, keeping to the east of Blackpool with the twin aim of protecting the new block from that side and finally helping Stilwell by attacking Mogaung from the south as he hit it from the north.

There is nothing like personal contact for clearing the air after weeks of communicating by garbled signals. Joe appreciated that my men should really be taken out after two slogging months of endless fighting, often in appalling conditions and always with the strain of knowing that we were behind the enemy lines and therefore on a hiding to nothing. But he called on us to make this final effort for the sake of the Chindits and to prove once and for all to the doubting Thomases that Wingate and the men who followed him had been right. Joe came up with me from Broadway to see my battalion commanders and brought some bottles of rum with him. That night, after he had gone, we lit a roaring fire up there in the Kachin Hills and drank the rum and sang our heads off as soldiers do, winding up with the last lines of the famous old battle song:

> 'Here's a toast to the dead already
> And here's to the next man to die.'

22

Vinegar Joe

Before General Lentaigne left us to return to his headquarters he passed on another item of news that was received by all with a certain amount of horror. For Lentaigne explained that, with the movement of the Chindit brigades northwards, we were all to come under the operational command of the American General Stilwell, who made no secret of his utter contempt for the British and who had certainly earned his nickname of 'Vinegar Joe'.

He was a powerful man in the South East Asia Command and held three important posts: Deputy Supreme Commander S.E.A.C., or in other words Mountbatten's number two; Commanding General of the American forces in the China-Burma-India theatre; and Chief of Staff to Chiang Kai-shek, his original job. Complicated Anglo-American politics seem to have been responsible for this situation and from the point of view of Allied co-operation and friendship it was a far from happy one. As far as I know Stilwell was an extremely capable general and at times he even seemed to succeed in overcoming his almost fanatical hatred of the British in the cause of a joint war effort. But there were numerous occasions when the demands and accusations he made while in command of the Chindits were beyond all reason and could only have come from a man who started off with an outsized bias.

However, at the moment we had other things than Vinegar Joe to worry about. The rains were starting and making movement more difficult along paths that had been covered with dust a few days before but were now slippery and would soon become knee-deep in mud. We met Claud Rome on May 15th and advanced, once more as a brigade, to the area around Lamai, east of Blackpool. From the hills there we could see the newly-installed block, across the valley through which the railway and the Namyin river ran, and we could hear the sound of gunfire as the Japs attacked it. The weather was appalling, with thunder roaring in competition with the Jap artillery and lightning flashing round the hills as the heavy rain streamed down. Even the sure-footed mules could not stay upright and they slipped and rolled down the jungle-covered slopes dragging supplies and equipment with them through the mud.

Our orders, nevertheless, were to protect the block from the east and I sent out the Lancashire Fusiliers, the South Staffords and the 3/6 Gurkhas on separate missions to clear the foothills of any enemy, to harass Jap transport in the valley and to attack any enemy gun positions they could find. The South Staffords were in action first. They crossed the valley and forced the Japs to move the guns that were shelling Blackpool from a place called Banmauk. The Fusiliers also cleared out some Japs but then the weather got even worse and the Namyin river came down in full flood, overflowing its banks and going at such a rate that, despite all our efforts, it was impossible to cross.

Meanwhile, over to the west, 14 Brigade had run into the enemy in the Kyusanlai Pass and had to fight there for the next five days before pushing the Japs back and continuing their march north. So the position was that neither my brigade nor 14 Brigade were able to help the unfortunate 111 Brigade at Blackpool.

Jack Masters, a first-class Gurkha officer who turned to writing after leaving the Army, was now in a jam. His rapid move northwards to install the block had been a model of jungle marching, but he was attacked by the enemy as soon as he arrived and had been under Jap fire ever since. Because of this Masters and his men, though they worked and fought like demons, never had the chance to prepare their defences properly, or to stock the block adequately with stores and ammunition. The weather, which had left us helpless on the other side of the racing waters of the Namyin and had delayed 14 Brigade even before they met the Japs, also brought supply by air to a halt at Blackpool and stopped the Mustangs providing close support. While dense cloud and torrential rain kept the planes away the Japs installed field artillery and anti-aircraft guns near the block. When the cloud lifted slightly a few days later several daring R.A.F. and U.S. pilots tried to drop supplies but were met by heavy ack-ack fire; on one mission eleven out of twelve transport planes were hit, and it was decided reluctantly that air supply attempts would have to be abandoned.

By now the battered, weary but still fighting 111 Brigade were isolated. They had no food left and little ammunition. Masters had no option but to evacuate. He carried this out expertly, despite the mud and the rain and the Japs, and the exhausted Chindits slogged their way to Mokso, where Masters had left some of his animal transport protected by a column of Gurkhas. His brigade had fought valiantly and had suffered 210 casualties in their stay at Blackpool; it must have been some consolation to them to know that the Jap casualties were more than twice that, about 500. Looking back, it is clear that 111 Brigade had been allotted an impossible task. Masters was told to site his block in an area which was too near the enemy's northern front in general, and the Jap garrison at Mogaung in particular. Whichever spot he had chosen he would have come under attack immediately simply because the Japanese had troops near at hand. This fact, plus the monsoon, meant Blackpool was doomed from the start.

While the battle for Blackpool was going on I was exchanging messages and information with Special Force H.Q. on my second objective, the advance towards and attack on Mogaung. I had sent some Gurkhas up to reconnoitre nearer the town and they reported back that it was held by about 4,000 Japs. Claud Rome and I agreed that our first essential was a firm base from which to launch our attack and that this should be as close to the town as possible. I then decided to send Claud up to join the Gurkhas and he left on May 26th, the day after Blackpool was evacuated. Anticipating orders from H.Q., I sent off the South Staffords as well, and prepared to follow on with the rest of the brigade. Soon afterwards the order came through for me to go for Mogaung as quickly as possible, form my own plan of attack and carry it through.

The weather was still filthy and we had quite a few chaps down with malaria; jungle sores were also on the increase in the humid, dripping atmosphere. These medical cases, plus a few wounded, meant we had stretchers to carry as well as the rest of our equipment and it was therefore a pleasant surprise when about eighty Oriya Indians, whom I have mentioned earlier, joined us after getting away from the Japs. They took over the stretcher-carrying and were a great help.

As we moved towards Mogaung we were often up to our knees in mud but we still made what I considered to be good progress. I was therefore amazed later on when I heard that General Stilwell had complained violently that we were moving too slowly and that I was deliberately disobeying orders. At the same time he also objected bitterly to the evacuation of Blackpool and wanted to know why other Chindit units had also been delayed. Joe Lentaigne did not pass on a word of this criticism to us in the field but took all of it on his own shoulders. Finally, however, Stilwell's bleatings reached Mountbatten's ears and he had to send Slim to the American's headquarters to smooth things over. In fact the situation was that Stilwell's Chinese troops had been held up by the weather and the Japs even more than we had; and the American commander, seeing that his plans were in danger of falling apart, mounted his favourite hobby horse and blamed the British. I also suspect that some of his staff officers, knowing his anti-British feelings, kept away from him highly relevant information about the Chindits so that the failure of their own troops would be less apparent. I will explain later my reasons for these suspicions.

We reached Wajit, about five or six miles from Mogaung, on June 1st. To add to our other discomforts we were now in bad leech country. When we stopped to rest we would find half a dozen or so on our legs, but I had discovered long ago that a sharp knock would dislodge them. Other men found the tip of a cigarette effective but I was a non-smoker and was hanged if I was going to start the tobacco habit just because of leeches. Around Wajit we had several skirmishes with Jap patrols, but we were not delayed unduly and joined up with Claud Rome at a village called Lakum on June 3rd. From our position, well dug-in along the ridge of a low hill, we could see Mogaung town about two miles away, and the plain we had to cross to reach it stretched out before us.

Although the big battle was now getting nearer we were all relieved to have arrived after the dreadful conditions on the journey. In some places, with our heavy packs on our backs, we had sunk up to our waists in mud and flood water. One Lancashire Fusiliers machine-gun crew, with their mules, slid all the way down a long slope and landed at the bottom among a lot of jabbering Japs, who were also bowled over. The fusiliers recovered first and took the necessary steps.

Three weeks and two days were to pass before we captured Mogaung. In many ways it was the worst three weeks of the war as far as I was concerned. The Chindits had not been trained or equipped for this type of fighting. An attack on a town is a job for a normal Army

Brigade complete with artillery and armoured support. We had no artillery, just our mortars, and the nearest British armoured vehicle was hundreds of miles away. We were the Chindits, the guerillas, the mobile marauders who were at the enemy's throat one minute and away the next looking for another target. We sat on Jap railway lines, ambushed Jap road convoys, raided their camps and supply dumps and skipped away again. And here we were, exhausted after three months behind the enemy lines, depleted in numbers by wounds, sickness and death, and with orders from a bitchy American general to take Mogaung.

In those three to four weeks 77 Brigade had nearly 1,000 casualties from battle and sickness. The average time for a subaltern to stay in one piece was three days and at the end there were hardly any of them left. At times I would feel like a butcher, and then I would see a man come out of our makeshift hospital with a wound only half healed and plead to be allowed back into the fight. The men knew what my orders were: to capture Mogaung. And we were the Chindits, the jungle fighters who took on the impossible and made it possible. We fought ourselves to a standstill and then we went on again with that extra bit of effort that wins battles. This was the spirit which finally carried us into Mogaung, the first town in Burma to be retaken.

We could never have come anywhere near success had it not been for the U.S. air force boys who supplied us with food and ammunition and acted as our artillery by bombing the Jap guns that were shelling us. Some of their light plane pilots also did wonders by landing on the air strip at our base just outside Mogaung and evacuating the seriously wounded. The dreadful soggy state of the so-called runway was enough to give any flier nightmares after one landing and take-off. But some of those chaps did it several times a day.

Typically enough, in the middle of all this, I was threatened with the sack over a matter that had nothing whatever to do with the conduct of the battle. The unwitting cause of the trouble was Captain Archie Wavell, whose father was now Viceroy of India. Archie led an attack which greatly strengthened our right flank near the Mogaung river, but he was hit in the wrist so badly that his hand was only just hanging on. He quickly applied a tourniquet and roughly bound his wound, then carried on until all his men were in their new positions.

It was a brave action and saved what might have been a dangerous situation. Later that night at our base medical unit the rest of Archie's hand was taken off and he was scheduled for flying out. I heard no more of him until I received a message at my forward H.Q. from General Lentaigne, the gist of which was that I would be relieved of my command immediately unless Captain Wavell was flown out that day. Apparently Lord and Lady Wavell, informed that their son had been wounded and was being evacuated, had flown up to Assam to meet him. But he had not arrived. I dashed back to the base area and discovered Archie still there: he had insisted that other men go out before he did. The plane kept coming back for him but he stuck to his guns, and more than sixty wounded men had gone out in this way. He probably saved the lives of many of them. In the end I had more or less to force him on to the plane.

I mention this because I was personally involved, but Archie's action was only one of endless acts of bravery and devotion during those dreadful weeks. Eventually the brigade collected two V.C.s[1] and dozens of other British and American awards for the battle of Mogaung, and I have no doubt that many deeds which should have been recognized were never reported.

A day or two after the threat to sack me another high-powered message arrived, this time from the Supreme Commander himself, Lord Mountbatten. It said: 'Convey to 77 Brigade my greatest satisfaction in splendid achievement of penetrating to Mogaung. This success after many weeks' hard fighting and marching shows clearly excellent fighting spirit of brigade to which I would like you to send my personal congratulations.' This bucked us up no end and I felt that Wingate would have been glad to see his original Chindit brigade receive such praise.

Of course, the staff boys were still at work and occasionally they would offer us advice. Among our other troubles was trench feet, caused by the appallingly wet conditions. We fought and lived most of the time in mud and water and everything and everywhere was at best damp and at worst soaking. It was most unpleasant to be sleeping

---

[1] Captain Michael Allmand and Rifleman Tulbahadur Pun, both of the 3/6 Gurkha Rifles won V.C.'s on 11th June 1944, during an attack on the bridge at Mogaung. Allmand's award was posthumous.

in a hammock in the middle of the night when the Japs opened up with their artillery, for it meant diving straight into a 3-foot-deep slit trench full to the brim with cold, muddy water. However, I felt that we could at least keep down the number of cases of trench feet by wearing gumboots, and sent a signal asking for 1,000 pairs to be dropped if it was possible to get hold of them. After a while a signal came back: 'It is the medical opinion that the wearing of gumboots injures the feet, and that the best insurance against trench feet is to keep the feet dry.' The staff boys never change.

For ten days we fought our way gradually forward but our losses were heavy. By June 13th the total attacking strength of the brigade had been cut down to 550 men, and this figure was being reduced daily not only by shelling and front-line attacks but also by malaria and other sickness. Of that 'fit' 550, many had been wounded once and most had had malaria during the past few weeks. For some time now we had been told that some of Stilwell's Chinese troops were on their way to help us and I knew we were rapidly reaching the stage when their arrival was essential if we were to keep going. I sent a signal to this effect to Joe Lentaigne and also asked Claud Rome to go out by air to see Joe and Stilwell, who promised to do all he could to speed up the Chinese.[2]

At last, on June 18th, the first batch of Chinese began to arrive and took over the vital task of protecting my exposed southern flank. Their presence was a great help and meant that I could concentrate more of my own men on the vital points of attack. This was just as well for I soon discovered that while the Chinese were quite happy to hold a position a frontal attack was not their cup of tea, though they got more used to the idea as the days went by.

We were very close now to taking the town but the Japs were fighting with great determination and courage. They had been reinforced from the area further north around Myitkyina, which incidentally relieved some of the pressure on Stilwell's troops held up there. We found that very few of the Japs ever gave in; they fought on until they were killed

---

[2] On 14th June I sent Captain Andrews of the Burma Rifles across the Mogaung River with the instructions not to return without at least one Chinese regiment. Four days later he appeared and announced that he had a Chinese regiment waiting on the bank of the river.

and there is no doubt that a well-trained Japanese soldier is a very tough customer indeed. In some sectors we had to fight almost for every yard and sometimes it was difficult to tell who was holding a particular spot at any given time. I joined in a charge on some Jap dug-outs by a mixed crowd of the Lancashire Fusiliers and the King's and we took the position after a brisk scrap. At twilight the fusiliers were cooking an evening meal in their newly won quarters when a patrol of seven men came in, slung down their rifles wearily and took off their equipment. One of the fusiliers looked up from the food and suddenly saw that the new arrivals were members of a Jap patrol who had not realized their position had been taken. There was a brief, close-quarters fight which the Lancashire lads won.

At this stage Mogaung was so nearly ours; the only question was whether we could muster the strength to make the last vital push. Even my brigade H.Q. personnel were now up in front under Major Gurling, the Animal Transport Officer, and they did a wonderful job. Some of them got right into Mogaung but were pushed back again and the Lancashire Fusiliers also got through at one stage, while on our left flank the Chinese were approaching the railway station. For the final effort I called on the ever-faithful 3/6 Gurkhas, now sadly depleted and all but exhausted. Freddie Shaw rallied his men and went forward, and they found surprisingly little opposition. The Japs had had enough at last and were withdrawing. On June 26th Mogaung was ours.

Those of us that were left could feel no elation. We had lost too many friends and too much strength to register any emotion at all. The one thing that did rouse us was to hear on the B.B.C. news an announcement, presumably put out by Stilwell's H.Q., that Chinese-American forces had taken Mogaung. I was nearly speechless.[3] But then the Chinese commander, Colonel Li, arrived at my H.Q. He, too, had heard the news and despite the fact that one of Stilwell's staff officers, an American lieutenant-colonel, was with me, Li said: 'If anyone has taken Mogaung it is your brigade, and we all admire the bravery of your soldiers.' He then bowed, saluted and left, ignoring the American.

---

[3] I could not resist sending a signal to Stilwell: 'The Chinese having taken Mogaung, 77 Brigade is proceeding to take Umbrage.' It is rumoured that Stilwell's staff officers searched in vain to find Umbrage on the map.

Colonel Li and I had got on well together since he had arrived a week before. He was an excellent soldier and although we had not always seen eye to eye on methods and tactics we had a good working arrangement and had shared the final victory. I knew the announcement was not his fault, which made me even more grateful for his unselfish action in apologizing for it in front of one of Stilwell's men. I am glad to say that Colonel Li was later awarded the O.B.E. and that two of his officers got the M.C.

It was now a month since I had sent the Gurkhas off from Lamai, which had been our first definite move towards Mogaung. In that month we lost seventeen officers and 238 other ranks killed, and thirty officers and 491 other ranks wounded. And those terrible figures did not include the men who were flown out sick, or those who died later in India. Nothing else seemed to matter much now, although we received messages of congratulation from Joe Lentaigne and his staff and from the other Chindit brigades, and they helped to cheer us a little. The one that meant most to many of us said simply: 'Wingate would have been proud of you.'

We left Mogaung to the Chinese and withdrew to our base area at Pinhmi, outside the town, to prepare for our withdrawal to India. Even the thought of this could not revive our sagging spirits. And then a message arrived from H.Q. ordering me to move down the railway to Hopin. I flatly refused. Signals began flashing back and forth rapidly. 'How many fit men have you?' I sent back: 'Three hundred.' My brigade had originally numbered more than 3,000. Even so I was asked to send those 300 down the railway and was told that they would not have to fight as there were not many Japs in the area; the only aim was not to lose the initiative gained by the capture of Mogaung. Or so they said.

I sent a long message to Joe Lentaigne because I realized I was putting him in a difficult position with Stilwell. I told Joe he could show Stilwell all my signals and I was prepared to take the consequences. But I would not ask any more of my men. Already reaction had set in among them and they were going down like flies with malaria, dysentery and other fevers. I was blaming myself for allowing them to be pushed so hard; if I had dug my toes in before perhaps our losses would not have been so heavy. With all this in my mind I was quite determined that they should not have to do any more, wherever the orders came from. I made this clear to Joe and said I was prepared to take any blame for not fighting. My men were past the limit of endurance.

All this took a day or two and in the middle of it Francis Stuart, who had fallen sick during the battle for Mogaung, was evacuated and promised to reinforce my arguments when he got to H.Q. I did not know it then but Francis had tuberculosis; he had had it throughout the campaign and I think he knew, though he told no one. He died a week or two later, but not before he saw Lentaigne. He was a loyal friend and colleague to the end.

Finally our orders came through to evacuate and we moved to Kamaing, then on up the Mogaung river to Shaduzup; from there planes took the brigade back to India. I disobeyed orders again, for we were supposed to go to Myitkyina, not Kamaing. But I was in a wretched state of mind by this time and suspected darkly that we were being sent to join in the fighting in the Myitkyina area. Looking back, I still feel justified for refusing to advance to Hopin; but my second bout of disobedience was totally wrong and I can put it down only to strain and exhaustion.

I was now able to report in person to Joe Lentaigne at his Advance H.Q. I had caused him a great deal of worry by my rebelliousness and the following morning we were to see Stilwell at his H.Q. in the jungle nearby. I gathered there was a possibility of a court martial but I was too weary to care. At that moment I was looking forward to sleeping under cover in a hut for the first time for four months; nothing else mattered much.

I was feeling rested but in much the same lackadaisical mood the next day. I sat one side of a table between Joe and his Colonel (Operations), Henry Alexander. Stilwell sat opposite me between two of his staff officers. I had decided to tell him, briefly, the whole story of 77 Brigade from the fly-in at Broadway to Mogaung. Then it would be up to him to do what he liked. We shook hands all round and the conversation started off something like this:

Stilwell: Well, Calvert, I've been wanting to meet you for some time.

Me: I've been wanting to meet you, too, sir.

Stilwell: You send some very strong signals, Calvert.

Me: You should see the ones my brigade major won't let me send.

Much to my amazement Stilwell roared with laughter at this. 'I have just the same trouble with my own staff officers when I draft signals to Washington,' he said.

From then on the whole atmosphere changed and it seemed almost as if Stilwell was on my side. That one remark, which might easily have upset him, had struck just the right chord. I reckoned it was the best stroke of luck I'd had for some time.

I found it easy after that to tell Stilwell the lot, and it gradually became pretty clear that some of his staff people had either seriously misled him or had not been doing their jobs properly. He punctuated my story with asides to his staff officers: 'Check that. Is it correct?' 'Yes, sir.' 'Why wasn't I told?' As his questions and answers went on it was obvious he had not realized we were the brigade that had flown in four months before. In view of this some of his demands and complaints did not seem quite so outrageous as they had done at the time.

There was no further mention of a court martial. Instead Stilwell said he would award the American Silver Star to five British officers.[4] Later I sent him five names but he ruled out one because most of that officer's gallant work had been before we came directly under Stilwell's command. He put my name down instead. So Stilwell made amends with me personally, though I understand he went on being his old vinegary self to a lot of other people, particularly if they happened to be British. I suppose it takes more than one isolated incident to change the hate of a lifetime.

We were now well into July and I went with the brigade to new quarters at Dehra Dun, north of Delhi, where there was a big yellow and black banner to welcome us: 'Chindits. Watch your saluting.'

Leave then, and I went to Ceylon for a glorious rest. Meanwhile 111 Brigade had come out of Burma soon after us and in August 14 Brigade and the West Africans were evacuated. By September I was back in Dehra Dun reforming 77 Brigade in preparation for a return to Burma, but a month or two later I busted my Achilles tendon playing football and had to fly to London to get it properly

---

[4] One of the officers was David Wilcox, one of the last surviving subalterns from the South Staffords. Wounded on four separate occasions he was personally put on a light plane by me and evacuated with a Jap bullet still embedded in his scalp.

fixed. It was wonderful to be home again but I had no thought of staying and chafed a bit as I hobbled around with my injured foot. A busted tendon takes a long time to put right and it seemed damn' silly to be put out of action with this after all the stuff I had missed in the jungle.

Then, to my utter dismay, I heard from India that the Chindits were to be disbanded and the re-formed brigades absorbed into the British and Indian forces advancing through Burma. I felt shattered, but it was pointed out to me that now the Japs were on the defensive and gradually retreating, our guerilla task was over. I felt that we could still do a useful job by getting behind the Japs and hastening the complete re-conquest of Burma. But without Wingate to fight for us I suppose it was inevitable that, once we had come out of the jungle, we would never be allowed back again as a special force.

Later Lord Louis Mountbatten wrote to me: 'It was the most distasteful job in my career to agree to your disbandment. I only agreed because by that time the whole Army was Chindit-minded.'

That made it all seem worth while.

23

Les Paras

While the Chindits were battling away against the Japanese in a forgotten corner of the Burma jungle great things were happening in Europe. We arrived outside Moguang on June 3rd; three days later the D-Day invasion forces landed in Normandy. Now, towards the end of 1944, Allied troops were driving the Germans through France and the Low Countries, back to the borders of the Fatherland. As I studied the news in London I realized that what I wanted was to get out there and join in. Once again my luck held, for as my convalescence came to an end I was offered the job of commanding the Special Air Service Brigade. This crack parachute force had been founded by David Stirling, whom I had known back in 1940 at Lochailort. But David was now a prisoner of war in Germany and I jumped at the chance of taking over.

The S.A.S. were stationed at Earls Colne, near Colchester in Essex, and I went down there in early January, 1945. I found that two British S.A.S. squadrons were already operating in Italy under Major Roy Farran, a very young and daring officer who won the D.S.O. and the M.C. and two bars, as well as French and American decorations, and later became well known for his exploits in Palestine after the war. Two other British S.A.S. regiments were at Earls Colne but not long after I took over I arranged for them to go on special duties with Second Army in France. While I was still responsible for these units my main task now was to take direct command of the rest of the brigade, totalling about 1,300 or 1,400 men: the Deuxième and Troisième Chasseurs Alpine Parachutiste, forerunners of the famous French 'Les Paras' who fought with great distinction later on in Indo-China and Algeria, and the 1st Belgian S.A.S.

Controlling this rough, highly-trained and sometimes rather wild

184

bunch of élite soldiers from France and Belgium was quite a proposition. Many of them had been in the Foreign Legion before making their way to England to join the Free French forces. Others had escaped from Occupied France after giving the Germans a run for their money with Resistance groups. In other words these men were not only first-class soldiers but also individualists with a lot of fighting experience behind them, and they were not prepared to accept any commander who happened to be put over them by higher authority. They were well disciplined, of course; but no one can command even trained and disciplined troops if he does not have their respect and confidence. The trouble was that I had little time in which to gain theirs.

Soon after I got to Earls Colne, and before I had had time to shake down properly, a complaint came in from a landowner – Lord Ullswater, a former Speaker of the House of Commons – that my men were shooting his hares and pheasants, using .303 ammunition. We had permission to train over part of his estate but shooting the game was strictly forbidden and I immediately issued orders that it was to stop. For a few days it died down, then another angry complaint bounced on to my desk. The whole thing had started again and there were threats that it would be taken up at Ministerial level.

The French, of course, were completely innocent. They assured me passionately and with much arm-waving that all their ammunition had been checked and none was missing, so how could they possibly be to blame? But I insisted on checking myself and demanded to see their store. Reluctantly they took me along to an old shed and there was their .303 ammunition – piled up anyhow in a corner! I was furious. They had not just disobeyed orders, they had lied to me, and I was determined they would pay for it whatever the cost to our relationship. I asked the battalion commander, Colonel Paris de Bollardière, to report to me with his adjutant and quartermaster, and all their staff. I was still in a rage and started off without any preamble:

'You told me all your ammunition was accounted for and I find this.' I pointed to the pile of .303 in the corner. 'Well, you've had your fun and now it's going to stop. I want every round of this ammunition counted and stacked so that it can be taken properly into store. And you'll all stay in here until the job's done.'

I stormed out and locked the door. It was quite early in the morning, about 9.30, when I locked them in. At six o'clock that evening I went to the shed, unlocked the door and found the .303 neatly stacked on newly made shelves. The French paratroops had even polished every round until the brass gleamed.

For a few days after that I waited with a certain amount of trepidation for these tough characters to get their revenge. But nothing happened. Indeed, I found that my whole job was suddenly becoming easier as Les Paras began to co-operate. It gradually dawned on me that my toughness over the hares and pheasants, which I had feared might finish me with the French altogether, had in fact earned me their respect. They were used to hard discipline and responded to it. From then on they gave me no trouble and de Bollardière and I became firm friends.

I had inherited a first-class Brigade H.Q. staff, which included Colonel Esmond Baring, of the Baring banking family, and Major L. E. O. T. (Pat) Hart, and they took a lot of the administrative burden off my shoulders in an extremely capable way. I also had a small tactical staff with British forward headquarters in Europe, liaising in the use of the S.A.S. regiments there, and I visited them several times during February in the light plane allotted to me. My main object was to find out whereabouts on the front my French and Belgians could be of most use. And finally, towards the end of March, it was decided we would go in on the left flank to help clear the Germans out of north-eastern Holland, east of the Zuider Zee.

The Allied advance had reached the Apeldoorn-Deventer area, north of Arnhem between the Zuider Zee and the Dutch-German frontier, and that part of the line was being manned by the Canadians with a Polish division nearby. The aim was for the French to drop in small parties at night over a wide area from Zwolle in the south to Groningen in the north and westwards out into the lake country of Friesland. The whole area, as with much of Holland, was crisscrossed with canals and bridges and one of our first essentials was to stop the Germans destroying the bridges over the main roads to Leeuwarden in the west and Groningen in the east. Once the parachutists had seized the key points the Canadians would advance north from Deventer and Apeldoorn to take over the area, pushing the Germans either out towards the North Sea coast or back towards their own frontier.

The planning went ahead swiftly. About forty points were chosen as dropping zones and I decided that the French would fly in, about 900 of them, while I stayed near the Canadian line with my tactical

H.Q. and the 400 Belgians in reserve. The time from the operation – known as Operation Amhurst – being first conceived to zero hour was six days, which I was told was something of a record for a combined air-ground effort of this size. The credit for this, I should add, goes largely to my wonderful H.Q. staff, which contained some of the best organizers I have ever seen.

Before the French took off from an airfield near Halstead in Essex, I gave a final briefing and it was exciting to feel the tension in the air. These men had been longing for action and now they were going to get it. They hated the Germans with the intensity that only the people of a conquered country can feel for the nation that has overwhelmed them. I almost felt sorry for the enemy soldiers who were going to meet these tough Frenchmen very shortly.

At the end of my briefing I decided that a little humour might relieve the strain so I took rather longer than necessary over my description of the type of country they would find. 'It's all pretty flat,' I said, 'and very largely farmland. I'm told there is also plenty of game to be had, such as hares and pheasants ...' They stared for a moment then broke out into cheers and roars of laughter. They were a gay crowd and their morale was terrific.

The drop took place at night and from early reports wirelessed back by the French to my headquarters near Deventer it clearly took the Germans by surprise. In a number of places we dropped dummy parachutists filled with all sorts of explosive devices which made noises like machine-guns, rifles, grenades and so on. A few of these could keep a German patrol on the hop for several hours with any luck; they really did sound most realistic and this little deception trick helped the French in a number of places that night. In fact Les Paras seemed to be thoroughly enjoying themselves from the cheerful tone of their signals back to us. Many of the Germans, for their part, put up no fight at all and one French corporal signalled for a supply of barbed wire to build a P.o.W. compound. He had eight men with him and they had taken 100 German prisoners, who were proving an embarrassment!

My main fear was that the Germans, worried about this sudden attack on an area which would give the Allies a foothold on the main road leading to Bremen and on up to Hamburg and Kiel, would throw in reserves to overpower the parachutists before the main force could overrun them and take over. That was why I had decided to hold the Belgians in reserve nearby, with their S.A.S. jeeps at the ready. These were fantastic vehicles, devised by David Stirling and his earlier S.A.S. colleagues. They were armoured, with a heavily protected radiator and bulletproof windscreen, and carried twin Vickers machine-guns in front and another behind. They had self-sealing petrol tanks, could lay their own smoke-screen and were tough enough to be dropped by parachute and be instantly ready for use. With four-wheel drive they would cross all types of country and proved their worth in many a fight.

I was also worried in case there was any eleventh-hour hitch in the Canadian plan to take over from the French. And my fears in this case were justified, though it was no fault of the Canadians. They were part of the main Allied line and had to work in co-operation with the rest of the front, and as luck would have it their armoured division was told at the last minute to advance eastwards in support of a similar move by other units south of them. This still left the Canadian infantry for the northward thrust towards Friesland and Groningen but I could see that some of my men, particularly those furthest north, would be on their own for a week or more unless I pushed into the area myself with the Belgians in their jeeps.

Four hundred men is not much of a force to take into a hostile area of that size, even if certain key places have already been captured by the advance party, as in this case. I therefore decided to fall back again on bluff, which had seen me through some difficult situations in the past. I had been lent a large, impressive-looking staff car and reckoned that most Germans would think twice before firing at it, simply because it was not the sort of vehicle one expected to see actually in action. And before they could realize they had been tricked the Belgians, following up, could deal with them.

It was a makeshift scheme which didn't bear too much thinking about so we put it into action before we could change our minds. I took a driver with me and one of my staff captains, a red-haired, French-speaking officer with the wonderful name of Potter Miller Mundy. We stuck a large Union Jack on the front of the car and set off, hoping for the best. I was already feeling a little more confident because we had also managed to take with us a Polish battery of self-propelled twenty-five-pounders, which would be invaluable if we hit a really determined bunch of Germans.

As we drove through the flat Dutch countryside Potter Miller Mundy and I were feeling pretty scared, to say the least. But to our amazement the plan worked like a charm. We would drive into a village and the Dutch, seeing this big British staff car and the Union Jack, would dash out to greet us. First among them would be the Resistance and they would quickly deal with any Germans who looked as if they might turn nasty; but most of the enemy troops surrendered to us. They were a pretty poor lot in most cases. The crack units were further south in the main battle areas and many of the ones we picked up were little more than occupation police.

The French parachutists were pleased to see us and I would leave a few of the Belgians at each place to reinforce them until the Canadians took over. At one village a French corporal rushed out to greet us, obviously relieved at our arrival, and got very excited when he saw me. *'Attendez, mon général, attendez!'* he shouted, and dashed back into a nearby house. A moment later he ran out again carrying something in his hand and with a tremendous flourish and a happy smile presented me with a pheasant!

In the countryside we did not meet with much trouble but at Assen, a town about fifteen miles from Groningen, we came up against stiffer opposition and the Polish gunners proved invaluable. Our toughest fight, however, came right at the end when we had nearly completed our relief task. About two hundred men of a German parachute battalion dug themselves in around a crossroads at a village just outside Groningen, on the highway leading due east from the town towards the German frontier. I imagine the German parachute troops were told that once this road fell the way would be open for the Britishers to thrust right into the Fatherland. And we soon found that they were a different proposition to most of the other enemy units we had come up against so far.

I called on the Canadians for air support and they sent in a squadron of fighter-bombers which plastered the German positions. Then I brought in the Polish gunners, who put 100 shells into the same area. Finally, under smoke cover and with their machine-guns blazing, the Belgians attacked and swept right over the enemy dug-outs. There were about 200 Germans originally, and by this time I had only about 100 Belgians with me, having dotted the rest around the countryside. But we took the position with just one casualty. It shows once again what close air support and artillery can do to soften up the enemy before an attack.

Apart from mopping-up operations the whole region was now under our control, with the Canadians following up rapidly. Seven days had passed since my Frenchmen had dropped in and General Sir Richard Gale, then Deputy Commander of the 1st Allied Airborne Army, congratulated us on the swiftness of the operation, which had not even been thought of a fortnight before. It meant, among other things, that Allied forces were able to cut off many German troops who had retreated up from the western side of Holland and crossed the big Zuider Zee causeway, hoping to reach safety in Emden. Altogether it was a tremendous achievement by the French and Belgians and I always felt they did not get the credit they deserved. It was reported briefly, but suddenly there seemed to be a clamp-down on information and soon the whole affair was forgotten. I was told later that at the time relations were strained – as they often were – between Prime Minister Winston Churchill and the Free French leader, General de Gaulle, and the British were determined not to publicize a French achievement. For my own part I thought they were magnificent and I managed to arrange, at a very high level, for Les Paras to be allowed to wear the British parachutists' red beret. They regarded this as a great honour and wore it proudly during their actions abroad after the war. Later I was awarded both the French and Belgian Croix de Guerre avec Palme, the French Legion d'Honneur (Officer) and the Belgian Ordre de Leopold II (Officer). But I have always regarded these awards as a tribute to the French and Belgians I commanded rather than to me personally.

For several days after the battle outside Groningen my men were scattered all over north-eastern Holland and at one stage we began to fear that our casualties in the original drop had been very high. But gradually the French trickled back into our re-forming area, many of them driving German vehicles, of all shapes and sizes. In their enthusiasm some of them had chased odd bands of enemy troops right back into Germany and had decided to return in comfort. Our final casualties were about thirty dead and thirty-five wounded.

We made our way back to the Deventer area and I travelled in a jeep with Colonel de Bollardière. We took a roundabout route to see some of the parts our men had liberated. But the driver took a wrong turning at one point and we must have inadvertently crossed the Dutch–German border, for much to our surprise we suddenly came upon an encampment surrounded by barbed wire and guarded by rather elderly German soldiers. The guards, who had obviously heard of our success a few miles away in Holland, surrendered with alacrity and flung open the gates for us. We drove slowly in, still a little dazed at this unexpected development. Then we heard shrill screams coming from inside the camp; we had been spotted by the prisoners, who rushed out to greet us. And within seconds we were being mobbed, hugged, kissed and nearly stripped by crowds of joyful girls!

In fact there were 6,000 Polish girls at the camp we had stumbled upon. They had been taken there after the tragic uprising in Warsaw the year before but they had not been badly treated, so they were fairly fit and undoubtedly man-hungry. Luckily I remembered that the Polish division was not far away and they let us go after we promised to send up the Poles immediately we reached them. We were in a pretty bedraggled state as we drove away from that camp. Our caps, badges and nearly all our buttons had been dragged off and our faces were scratched as if we had been in a rough house rather than a happy liberation demonstration. I told de Bollardière that I would rather face the German parachutists again than drive back into that camp alone, but he was a Frenchman and I don't think he entirely agreed. '*C'est la guerre,*' he said and shrugged, but there was a gleam in his eye.

We reached the Polish Division soon afterwards. They were startled at our appearance but we told them of our find and I have rarely seen men move more quickly. At the camp they wanted to kill all the German guards and wardresses at once, but the girls stopped them. They pointed out those who had treated them well and they were taken prisoner. The rest, the brutal ones, were taken out and shot. Summary jurisdiction, perhaps, but no more so than the Germans exercised themselves in Poland.

For a time after that there was something of a dent in the Allied line while the Poles and the girls had a tremendous reunion beano. Having seen those girls in action, I imagine it must have been quite a party. And the revitalized Poles soon made up for lost fighting time when they returned to the war!

24

East and West

Soon after we returned to Earls Colne from Holland the war in Europe ended and the German surrender was signed. The Government decided that victory should be celebrated on VE Day, May 8th, 1945, and there were parades and speeches, singing and drinking, music and dancing and also sadness and tears for those who would never come home. Meanwhile, many problems and unanswered questions remained. One of them concerned the reaction of the many thousands of German troops in Norway. No doubt they had been ordered to obey the terms of surrender. But would they? The Special Air Service and the 1st Airborne Division were ordered to fly there immediately to find out.

The French and Belgians were due to return to their own countries but I now had under command the two British S.A.S. regiments, totalling about 1,000 men, who had returned to Earls Colne from Second Army. The plan was for us to be flown into Stavanger by transport aircraft, along with the parachute boys, on the day after VE Day. We would be the first British troops to land in Norway in force since the evacuation in 1940, when I had been one of the last out at Andalsnes. Various plans had been put forward in the intervening years to make a large-scale Allied landing in Norway but they had come to nothing, and the Norwegians had suffered more than four years of German occupation. As for the enemy forces there, they were a long way from home and some of the more fanatical ones might try a suicidal last stand. Information from Norwegian sources suggested all would be well and we hoped it would be, but we were prepared for trouble.

I took off from an airfield in Essex with an advance party of five officers and thirty men, plus our vehicles. The weather was bad on the way and soon after we landed it closed down completely, bringing all further flying to a halt for the time being. A few other planes had managed to get in but they were all carrying the Airborne chaps, who were going to take over the Stavanger and Oslo zones. My orders were to travel south and assume control of Kristiansand and the surrounding area. At Stavanger, which the 1st Airborne Division took over with no trouble at all, we were told the weather might remain nasty for several days so I decided to take a chance and go on with the advance party alone.

The Norwegians greeted us joyfully as we drove down the south-western tip of Norway to Kristiansand, which is about 150 miles from Stavanger. The Germans stared sullenly but showed no inclination to fight and we began to feel more confident. As we entered Kristiansand, however, we saw so many Germans about that we felt they might shoot us down at any moment and I wondered if we had walked into a trap. But again, much to our relief, they showed no signs of fight, although from the point of view of numbers we were completely at their mercy.

At the German Army headquarters in the centre of the town I found the commanding officer – a lieutenant-general – and his staff co-operative and only too willing to obey orders and surrender to me. It was quite amazing to us to see the proud Germans, who had strutted arrogantly around Europe for so long, reduced to this submissive role. I suppose, after the tremendous build-up Hitler had given them as the Master Race, their defeat in battle and final surrender had come as a shattering blow. In Norway the German Army was completely demoralized and only too willing to give up; they all seemed thankful to have got out of the war alive.

However, I had little time to dwell on the psychological aspects of defeat. I was rapidly learning that victory can present the conquerors with some nasty headaches. Apart from several thousand German troops, there were about 40,000 Russian prisoners of war in camps in the Kristiansand zone, twenty-six German U-boats in the harbour along with more than a quarter of a million tons of surface shipping, and a Luftwaffe unit at an airfield nearby. As I grasped these figures I began to feel apprehensive again as I thought of the tiny party of men I had at my disposal. How on earth could thirty-six of us control all this lot until the rest of the chaps arrived? I decided I would have to put on an act, pretending I was completely ruthless and confident, though I certainly did not feel it.

I demanded to be taken to the German naval headquarters in the town. On the way there I roared at any German who didn't salute me and ordered the German officers to see that the offenders were arrested, which they did. All this nonsense had the desired effect and even the naval officers, who were made of sterner stuff than most of the army staff, finally agreed to surrender to me, though they made it plain they did so under protest and considered that a British naval officer should have been present. The Luftwaffe pilots were even more difficult and seemed to consider themselves a cut above the other two arms of the service. They offered no opposition and obviously realized the futility of a last-ditch fight now that the Germans everywhere else had given in. But they ignored us as far as possible and for the time being I left them to it; they would have to be brought into line sooner or later but it could wait until the rest of my men arrived.

As it was I was hard put to it to find enough guards even for the vital points, such as the various service headquarters, the harbour and so on. For instance, the twenty-six U-boats were all of the latest type and fitted with the Schnörkel breathing tube and air-intake device, which enabled them to stay under water for long periods without having to surface at night, as ordinary submarines had to do. During the last few months these newly-converted Schnörkel subs had been giving the Royal Navy a lot of trouble and twenty-six of them in one batch was quite a bag, even for the Army! But I could only spare one man to guard them. When he went on duty he would count them to make sure they were all there, like a farmer checking his sheep. It was a crazy situation and in fact one of the U-boats got away; later, I understand, it turned up in the Argentine. But the remaining twenty-five were handed over safely to the Navy when they arrived some time later, after clearing the thickly laid minefields at the harbour entrance and in the coastal waters.

The Russians were another problem. Through interpreters they told me that the Germans had made a point of shooting all Soviet officers. A few claimed that they had managed to get rid of their uniforms and pretend they were other ranks and I had to accept what they said, for the time being anyway, as I had no means of checking and the camps needed leaders. They had kept their quarters in good shape, which was just as well, for there was nowhere else for them to go. Ships could not reach us because of the minefields so I called for supply drops of food and clothing for the Russians as one of my first priorities, and they were extremely grateful when these eventually arrived.

For five days our small party grappled with these and many other tricky problems. Then the weather cleared and the rest of my S.A.S. men began arriving and eased the strain. I was able to leave more of the details to the civil affairs officers who had come over with us and they soon got down to the job of helping the Norwegians reorganize the normal civilian life of the zone, though it was a slow process after so long. Meanwhile, the 1st Airborne were gradually spreading across the country towards Oslo, rounding up the Germans and liberating towns and villages. After a few weeks I was ordered to take over Bergen zone which was about the size of Wales. Part of the 1st Airborne would take over the smaller Kristiansand zone from me.

I was beginning to feel that I could have done with rather less training in fighting and more in politics and diplomacy. As zone commander I had wide powers, but I also had to tread warily. For instance, not all the Norwegians liked the British, and I suppose some of them had good reason. There were huge submarine pens in Bergen harbour which the Germans had used to refit U-boats, and a year or so before they were selected as the target for a special bombing raid by the R.A.F. Unfortunately there was a school very near to the pens in the harbour area; this was known and repeated broadcasts were made prior to the raid, warning the Norwegians to keep the children away. Either they did not hear these warnings or ignored them, for the school was full when the raid took place. The R.A.F. used giant 20,000 lb. bombs to penetrate and wreck the submarine pens; one of them just missed the target and hit the school. All 300 children inside were killed. It was a tragic accident of war but, not unnaturally, it left some bitterness.

On another occasion there were complaints about a dance held in a warrant officers' and sergeants' mess in Bergen. The trouble was that I had given them the building where the Gestapo headquarters had been, and all this gaiety going on in a place where Norwegians had been tortured and died hurt some feelings. Again, this was understandable, and I had to explain that no disrespect had been intended. Sometimes I longed to be back in action, where the issues were more straightforward.

In Bergen we had the same trouble with minefields as in Kristiansand, and it took several weeks for the Navy's minesweepers to clear a safe channel into the harbour. There were also mines on the beaches and as the Germans had put them there it seemed only right they should remove them. After a squad had declared a beach mine-free they were made to link arms over the whole width of the beach and start walking. Once or twice a mine that had been left behind blew up as they went over it, killing or injuring two or three men. We found this was a good way of ensuring that none were deliberately left behind to kill more Norwegians; enough had died already at German hands.

The commanding officer of the Germans in Bergen was Lieutenant-General de Boer. We had regular meetings during which I passed on my orders to him, and these exchanges were extremely formal and correct, or at least they should have been. De Boer was always accompanied by his A.D.C., a tall, blond Nazi of the worst type. My A.D.C. at that time was Roy Farran, who had now joined us with his two squadrons from Italy. I remember that one of these meetings took place the day after we had had a particularly hilarious guest night in the mess. At one stage during the evening Lieutenant-Colonel Paddy Maine, a giant of a man who played rugger for Ireland and won no less than four D.S.O.s, had heaved me over his shoulder; my forehead came into contact with a fender and I ended up with two huge black eyes. The next day de Boer's A.D.C. kept looking at me and sniggering behind his hand and although I was not particularly worried I noticed that Roy Farran seemed rather fidgety. When de Boer and the A.D.C. left the room Roy went out with them and almost at once I heard a racket going on in the ante-room outside my office. Then the door opened and Roy returned.

'Excuse me, sir,' he said. 'The general would like another interview with you tomorrow.'

I thought something odd was going on but decided to wait and see what happened. The following day de Boer arrived with his young Nazi, who looked extremely crestfallen. He, too, was now sporting two black eyes and a glance at Roy Farran's beaming face told me how he had got them.

As I have already indicated, a tremendous number of Russian prisoners of war were taken to Norway by the Germans. There were numerous camps around Bergen alone with getting on for 60,000 Russians inside them. I had two Russian-speaking officers with me and we did all we could to make the ex-prisoners comfortable. Apart from providing them with clothing and food I opened canteens for them in the towns and tried to bring a little joy into their lives. We had been in Bergen about three weeks when a Soviet military mission arrived to take over the Russian prisoners. The mission was commanded by an English-speaking major called Sorokopud. At first he was suspicious but soon he loosened up and we got on quite well together. He was slightly disconcerted because some of the Russians had a habit of singing 'God Save the King' whenever I visited their camp, presumably as a gesture of thanks for what I had done for them. But Sorokopud was a soldier at heart, as I am, and we could forget politics when we felt like doing so.

This happy state of affairs didn't last for long. Two or three weeks behind Sorokopud and his notary mission came the Russian commissars. It is difficult to explain the effect they had on me when they first entered my office. There was nothing fearful-looking about them, but somehow they seemed to exude an air of evil. This may sound melodramatic but it sums up what I felt. It did not take long, however, for anger to replace revulsion. For these slimy characters accused me of ill-treating the Russians in the camps and, an even worse sin in their eyes, subjecting them to Western influence. I told them they were talking nonsense and took them on a personal tour, which lasted all day. I was so furious that I kept them on the move for hour after hour, from one camp to the next, without a break of any kind, even for lunch. They wilted somewhat towards the end but the next morning they bounced right back, as Communists do *ad nauseam*, with precisely the same accusations. I told them that as a soldier I was used to obeying orders even if I considered them nonsensical, and it was clear to me they were doing just that. Therefore I could waste no further time with them. I would willingly see them again if they had something constructive to discuss but I was too busy to listen endlessly to the same ridiculous string of complaints.

After this, I regret to say, we started having trouble in the Russian camps, stirred up by the poisonous commissars. They started giving political lectures, ramming home the Red line, and everyone in the camps was forced to attend. There were a few Poles who had either volunteered for the Red Army or been chain-ganged into it, and they objected to the indoctrination sessions. That was one of the causes of friction. Another was that some of the Russians themselves wanted to stay in Norway, or somewhere in the West, instead of going home. They were got at by the agitators and strong-arm squads formed by the commissars and there was more trouble. The way those camps deteriorated after the arrival of the Communist Party toughs was an object lesson to me in the methods of the Reds. Nothing would have pleased me more than to take in a few of my S.A.S. chaps to sort them out but even I, an infant in the world of politics, realized that this would be madness.

Gradually the situation in Norway began to return to normal, or as normal as it could be with so many Russian, German and Allied troops about the place. The Norwegian leaders in Oslo, many of whom had spent the last few years in England, were once again taking up the reins of government. In the big towns mayors and other civic officials were settling back into their jobs.

Towards the end of the summer I put arrangements in hand for a big parade through Bergen on Allied Forces Day. Invitations went out to all arms to send contingents and bands were arranged, a route laid out and so on. The Russians, of course, had been our allies during the war and an invitation went to them automatically. We heard nothing from them and though we checked several times they either could not or would not reply. Since the commissars arrived we had got used to this sort of reaction and decided to go ahead without them.

As zone commander I was to take the salute, standing on a dais in the middle of a wide street in the middle of Bergen, rather like Whitehall. The Royal Navy had been with us for some time, together with some ships of the Royal Norwegian Navy which had been fighting with the Allies. With all these, plus the R.A.F. chaps who had taken over the airfields, my own men and other army units now in the area, we had several thousand men for the parade.

The big day came. On the dais with me, apart from one or two staff officers, was a vice-admiral on a visit to his men in Bergen. And on the pavements were thousands of Norwegians out for the day to look on and enjoy the fun. Gradually the sound of the leading band drew nearer and down the road I could see the first contingent in the parade, from the Royal Norwegian Navy, swinging towards us. Then suddenly Colonel Baring gripped my arm and whispered urgently in my ear: 'My God, Michael, the Russians are coming the other way!'

I turned my head so quickly I nearly cricked my neck. Sure enough another and completely unexpected parade was approaching the dais from the opposite direction, and it could only be the Russians. What had happened was anybody's guess. Perhaps the commissars had forbidden the Russian soldiers to take part but had been defied; perhaps they had decided they could not march in the same parade as decadent Westerners but would stage their own. Anyway here they were, and it looked as if there were thousands of them.

I was in quite a spot. If I took the salute from our own parade I would have my back to the Russians and that was unthinkable; it was also impossible for me to take the salute from the Russians and ignore the others. Then I spotted the admiral and realized the situation could be saved. He agreed to cope with our parade while I faced the Russians. And that is what we did, standing back to back on the dais.

Everybody took it in good part and after the first shock we all found it quite amusing, if slightly chaotic. Unfortunately there was now a British headquarters with the usual collection of staff officers in Oslo. They soon got to hear of our little local difficulty in Bergen and demanded a written explanation from me of what they called a disgraceful incident which held us up to ridicule. General 'Bulgy' Thomas was C.-in-C. and it was not he who drafted the signal.

I started to draft out my reply, saying exactly what had taken place and denying that it was anything like a 'disgraceful' incident. I explained that this was the sort of thing that was always liable to happen when dealing with the Russians, then it occurred to me that I was wasting my time and merely pandering to these staff chaps. I threw my draft away and sent a signal containing thirteen words:

'East is east and west is west and never the twain shall meet.' I never heard any more about it, so presumably the quotation had the desired effect, though I did not realize just how true those words would prove to be during the years to come. The war I had started preparing myself for back in the early nineteen-thirties was over. But another struggle for power had already begun. And these two parades, staring straight ahead and moving in opposite directions, one from the East and one from the West, just about summed up what it was all about.

25

Who Dares Wins

The East has a nasty habit of catching up with people who have spent a long time out there. It caught up with me in Bergen in the shape of a very bad bout of malaria, and I had to come home for treatment in the late summer of 1945. By then the atomic bombs had been dropped on Hiroshima and Nagasaki and the Japanese had surrendered. The war was over.

I wondered what would happen to me. For the past few years I had either been preparing to fight, fighting or recovering from fighting. And there was no doubt about it, I was a fighting man. The fact remains that in peacetime a man born to battle has to change his ways, and this I had to face.

I was therefore very glad when, a few months later, I was sent back to India to take charge of the Royal Engineers with the 1st Indian Armoured Division at Secunderabad. In India, in those days, even peacetime had a certain edge to it and I felt that this would help to break me in gently to my new life. Later on the powers-that-be decided to make a new postwar appreciation of India's defences and I was sent on a reconnaissance around the border with Persia and Afghanistan, along the wild and beautiful north-west frontier. I travelled light, camped where I pleased, did some shooting between working on my reports and thoroughly enjoyed myself. If this was peacetime, I felt, I might even take to it. But, of course, my trip could not go on forever.

In this book I have not tried very hard to hide my feelings about certain types of staff officers. I have known, worked with and been very grateful to some excellent ones over the years. The sort that really send the man in the field round the bend are, fortunately, very much in the minority, but they tend to stand out because of their crass stupidity; this leads sensible men to curse all staff officers, which is really unfair. Nevertheless I felt distictly uneasy when my next posting came through; I was to spend a year studying at the Staff College at Camberley. However, I realised that this was an essential part of my army career and I learned a lot, though I couldn't help arguing now and then. When I left Camberley I was given a fullblooded staff job, on the Exercise Planning Staff of the Chief of the Imperial General Staff. The C.I.G.S. at that time was Field Marshal Lord Montgomery, whose flower pots I had blown up in Kent eight years perviously.

I found Monty a good man to work for. He did not suffer fools gladly and liked to be obeyed, but he hated sycophants. At dinner one day a number of generals and other high-ranking officers were at the table and Monty, well known for his abstinence, asked each of them if they would like a drink. They all refused. 'What about you, Calvert?' 'I'll have a pint of beer, sir.' Monty looked round the table and said, 'Thank God somebody tells the truth.' I could feel the knives in my back.

Towards the end of 1948 I was sent as Planning and Advisory Officer to the Allied Military Government in Trieste, which was then a free zone. I wrote reports for governments and the United Nations on all sorts of subjects, headed a boundary commission which sorted out some border troubles and generally felt that I was becoming a true staff wallah myself.

In 1950 I was sent back to the East again, to Hong Kong, which had been my first overseas posting in 1936. This was another staff job but already I was beginning to smell trouble again, for by now the communist rebels in Malaya were becoming a major problem.

I took over the job of G1 Air and was training troops bound for Korea in the use of air support, when I received a summons to report to General Sir John Harding, the Commander-in-Chief Far East, in Singapore. He told me he wanted somebody who knew about jungle fighting to produce a report on how to beat the rebels, and Slim, who was now C.I.G.S. had suggested me. The time limit was six months.

The communist insurgency in Malaya had begun two years earlier on the morning of 16th June 1948, when three young Chinese shot dead a rubber plantation manager in the northern town of Sungei Siput. Two other planters suffered the same fate half an hour later and ten miles away. Soon, five thousand Communist guerillas were under arms and operating from secret jungle camps. Ranged against them were around 4,000 British and Malay fighting men, few with any jungle experience.

The trouble was, the guerrillas could strike without warning and disappear before troops or police reached the scene. During 1950, 646 civilians had been murdered and 106 were missing. No one was spared, whether they be police, soldiers, rubber tappers and their families, or the white planters themselves. One of the early aims of the guerrillas was to strike terror into the native Malays and the thousands of Chinese who moved into the country during the war. And this they did with great success.

The fighting was a battle of wits more than strength. The rebels were full of guile, darting into the attack, then vanishing into the dense cover of the jungle. Many of them had been trained by the British Force 136 during the war and were equipped with arms parachuted to them years before with which to fight the Japanese.

On one of my trips my driver and I were moving at a fair pace along a jungle road when a burst of machine-gun fire came from the thick bush, slightly ahead of us. We jerked to a halt and flung ourselves into a ditch by the side of the road. For the first time in more than five years I was under enemy fire and when a grenade landed neatly beside me in the ditch I thought it was for the last time. I snatched up the grenade, hoping to be able to throw it out before it went off, and then I noticed that the pin was still in position. A piece of paper was attached to it and a scrawled message said; 'How do you do, Mr Calvert?' It could mean only one thing. Somebody I had known, and probably trained, in the old days in Hong Kong or in Burma, was now on the other side, fighting for the Communists!

For the next six months I travelled extensively all over Malaya. I visited ornate palaces and asked the views of wealthy sultans. I went to brothels and picked up the gossip of the gutter. I had myself put in jail in disguise and rubbed shoulders with captured Communists. I went on tours of the jungle on my own and I joined anti-rebel patrols of British troops in the jungle.

Most of the troops were national servicemen with little or no jungle experience. The doctors said that they could not live in the jungle for more than one week. Many of the officers had no experience of jungle fighting; they had been taken prisoner of war at places like Dunkirk and Singapore and were released at the end of the war. The conscripted men and officers who had fought in the jungle with 14th Army or the Chindits had long ago returned to civilian life.

Every time I went on patrol I sent a report back to General Harding, detailing the types of mistakes they were making. Units had gone back to the pre-Burma days of communal cooking, so they could not go out on small patrols and cook for themselves. They had fourteen pound tins of bully beef and I recommended the introduction of two pound tins. There was also no resupply by air at that time.

I went down to a light infantry battalion and met a company commander who had come up through the ranks. A very energetic chap with a very good company and I taught them how to put down ambushes. Normally an ambush only kills the first two or three men as you cannot see the others, so I taught them to lay instantaneous fuse right down the path, attached to hand grenades, so that when they saw the first man, they'd blow it up and get some of the people in the rear.

They'd man these ambushes for up to a week at a time, just two people on the trigger with the others resting. We found some guerrillas and drove them down in the direction of the ambushes and we had three very successful ambushes in which a number were killed and we were at the peak of our success when the company commander said to me, 'Sorry Sir, but I've got to go.' I said, 'What do you mean you've got to go?' He said 'The battalion commander said that its guest night on Thursday and all officers will attend or leave the regiment.' So we had to pack up. I went and saw Harding and he was horrified and furious about this.

I went on another patrol with a different regiment. They were told to patrol from one point to another and I discovered that the Army was not being taught how to patrol on its feet. They used to be able to do it during the war, but now they just hacked their way through the jungle in a straight line, from one point to another, making a lot of noise and achieving very little.

I suggested that they go out on patrols, not in a section or platoon, but just a few men at a time. The fewer you are in a patrol, the more frightened you are, therefore the more cautious and silent you are, therefore you are more likely to meet the enemy. And that was the object there. The battalion commander listened to this and suddenly he blew up and said, 'My regiment was raised and trained to fight in

Europe and I am not going to change my organisation and training just to chase a few bare-arsed niggers around South East Asia.'

Shortly afterwards I saw Harding for the third time and I was tired out and said, 'It is absolutely hopeless Sir.' He asked me 'What is hopeless?' I told him the story, leaving out the name of the officer and the unit. He said to me, 'Give me the name of the officer.' I said, 'If you remember Sir, I said when I first came out that I'd give you the reports, but I would not name names.' He put on his hat and called in his chief of staff and said, 'Colonel Calvert, I am giving you a direct order. Tell me the name of the officer.' I did so and he turned to his chief of staff and said, 'Tell him to come and see me tomorrow with a packed suitcase.' He came and was sent home to England.

I went out on a patrol with the Gurkhas and they were very energetic, but again they didn't seem to patrol very well. We laid an ambush one day and the guerrillas approached, but turned back and went away. I could not think why. I went up the path and there in the mud was a Gurkha footprint. One of them had gone off to scavenge or do something and had disobeyed orders and walked across the path. The footprint had alerted the guerrillas that something was amiss, so they turned around and disappeared whence they came. It was most disappointing as we had been laying in ambush for a week.

When the six months were up I made my official report, which comprised ten or twelve points. A number of these were included in what became known as the Briggs Plan, put forward by General Briggs, the Director of Operations at that time. These included the idea of resettling the tens of thousands of Chinese squatters in fortified villages, to prevent them assisting the guerrillas. One main point that I made was the need for 'One man, with one plan and with the power to carry it out.' The Army, Police, civil authorities and the Sultans were all pulling in different directions. They needed one man in charge and one plan that they could all follow.

I was flown to England and met the minister for the colonies and asked whom did I recommend? My first suggestion was Casey, the Governor of Bengal and later Governor of Australia. A very good chap. However, they said no, no, it must be someone English and in the services. I thought a bit and said, 'The man I'd hate most to have against me if I was a guerrilla, because he is ruthless and has got charm and is highly intelligent, is General Sir Gerald Templer.'

Prime Minister Churchill sent him to Malaya in February 1952, armed with military and political powers greater than any British soldier had enjoyed since Cromwell.

Another important recommendation that I made, which would have a far reaching effect on the special operations capability of the British Army, was the formation of a force that would live, move and have its being in the jungle, like the guerrillas. They should be able to operate in the jungle for up to three months at a time, supplied and supported by air. This suggestion was approved and I was told to form a force. The name I chose for the new unit was the Malayan Scouts (Special Air Service Regiment) and its role was to operate in deep jungle areas not already covered by other security forces, with the object of destroying guerilla forces, their camps and sources of supply.

The members of the new unit would still wear their own regimental head-dress and badges, but with the shoulder title 'Malayan Scouts' on their standard issue olive green uniforms. The arm flash was a shield with 'The Malayan Scouts' scrolled at the top; a Malayan Kris (knife) through a set of blue wings below which was the abbreviation S.A.S. We would come under the direct command of the GOC.

Gaining approval for the new unit was a far easier task than raising the new organisation. I was not allowed to pick and chose my Other Ranks. I sent a request for volunteers to all of the Army battalions in Hong Kong and Malaya, but I had to let the battalion commanders choose the men and send them to me. Some chose to off-load their unruly elements on me and whilst I could RTU them (return to unit), I was not allowed to pick them. I was allowed to pick and choose officers, but only from South East Asia; Hong Kong and Malaya. This was in many ways due to the very big anti-Chindit element amongst the former Indian Army officers, dating back to the Burma days.

By the middle of August 1950 I had recruited enough men and officers to form 'A' Squadron, Malayan Scouts (SAS). However, I had to try to form the new regiment from scratch, with inadequate administrative staff and accommodation. I was also faced with the small matter of training the men in the techniques of jungle fighting.

In an attempt to make things more realistic I used to send the men into the jungle in pairs, armed with air rifles and wearing fencing masks. They would stalk each other and could happily shoot the other without causing too much damage. General Harding came out one day with an

Australian General, saw the men shooting each other and asked if it hurt. I told one of the men to shoot at me and it did sting. Harding said 'Now have a shot at me' and he took a few shots without a murmur. Then he made the Australian stand there and be shot too.

We trained around Jahore and one of the things we practiced a lot was throwing grenades. You cannot bowl grenades over arm in the jungle in case it hits a branch and bounces back at you, so for PT every morning before breakfast we would go into the jungle and practice throwing grenades as you would a stone.

I took the whole unit into the jungle near Ipoh in the north of Malaya and occupied an old guerrilla camp. By actually living there we learned a hell of a lot about the enemy and went out on patrols from there. We did not kill any guerrillas in action, but we did leave behind exploding bullets and grenades with instant fuses, which would kill anyone when they tried to use them.

I wanted my men to think for themselves and not act on orders. To open fire on ambushes and not wait for an officer to tell them. Often in the jungle in Burma Japs would sail right through an ambush because the men were waiting for orders to fire. When you meet a guerrilla in the jungle you have to take snap shots as soon as the opportunity presents itself and the men were not used to that.

One of my better acquisitions was Captain John Woodhouse who was serving as G3 Intelligence to 40th Infantry Division in Hong Kong. He agreed to join me on the strict proviso that he would go out on operations as a troop or squadron commander. I agreed and on his arrival made him our intelligence officer. John was an excellent intelligence officer, just what we needed at the time. He eventually became one of the best commanding officers the 22nd SAS Regiment ever had.

I tried to get helicopters to work with us, for resupply or casualty evacuation, but the Army and Air Force said there were none available. So I wrote to Lady Mountbatten who was head of the Red Cross and she contacted Lord Mountbatten, who got us Navy helicopters. We carried out tests on the size of the landing zones required to land a helicopter in the jungle and our first operations were supported by Navy helicopters before the RAF stepped in and told us that they did have helicopters available after all.

In September 1950 Rhodesia offered a token force of men for service in Malaya. There was no shortage of volunteers and they were soon training at King George VI Barracks in Salisbury. In January 1951 I travelled to Rhodesia to take them under my wing. It was a long journey from Malaya to Rhodesia and back. I flew to Cairo, then to Nairobi where I gave some lectures and then I worked my way down Africa to Rhodesia. On the way back I was given the chance of going on a Thai warship which intercepted and caught a boat taking arms to Malaya, something which the Royal Navy insisted was not going on.

I was very impressed with the men and they became 'C' Squadron (Rhodesia) The Malayan Scouts (SAS) and arrived in Singapore in March 1951. I was glad to have them. They were commanded by a Captain Peter Walls, who later became a General and commander of his country's Army.

Before the Rhodesians arrived a ready made squadron was sent out from England to become 'B' Squadron, The Malayan Scouts. This was 'M' Independent Squadron from the Territorial Army reserve unit, the 21st SAS Regiment (Artists Rifles). Many of its men were former wartime SAS members and they were not very impressed with the lack of discipline amongst the men of 'A' Squadron. I must take the blame for much of this, including the fact that the men of my original squadron wore beards both in and out of the jungle. Wearing a beard in the jungle as the Chindits used to, was preferable to shaving daily, where water may be scarce and any cuts would soon become infected. Allowing the men to keep their beards when they came out, to the outrage of the military police and the resentment of other units, was clearly a mistake.

In my defence I must say that I had so much to do that some minor problems escaped me. I was serving three different Generals, Urqhuart who was GOC Malaya, Harding and Briggs, a wise old man who wanted me to advise him on the Briggs Plan. I attended high level meetings while still having to attend to people brought up in front of me for the loss of a pair of boots or something. I had asked for a quartermaster but they did not send one for a long time.

Some French Foreign Legionnaires jumped ship in Singapore and they were sent to me as possible recruits. They were quite useless, but it was an example of the diversions that I had to deal with, while trying to form, train and operate the unit without the officers or admin staff to assist me.

207

Most of the newly arrived 'B' Squadron were good men, and when 'D' Squadron soon followed from England I made John Woodhouse their new commander.

In June 1951 I found myself in the British Military Hospital in Kinrara for 12 days, suffering from 'Hepatomegaly of unknown origin.' The doctor's notes read 'Previous history of case; had dysentery in China 1937 – self treated. Recurrent diarrhoea 1946 in India. Treated with three courses of emetine in England 1947. Further proved amoebic dysentry in Trieste 1949. After that was symptom free till six months ago.' The rest of the details are not for the faint hearted, but the bottom line was that my insides were in a frightful state. On 22nd June I was flown to the British Military Hospital in Singapore and thence to the UK as a Class 'A' invalid to the Queen Alexandra Military Hospital in London.

I was eventually given two months sick leave and by October felt better than I had done for years. However, a change of scene from the jungle was in order and I was sent out to Germany, to join the British Army on the Rhine as CRE (Commander Royal Engineers) in Hannover. There was good news from Malaya though; the designation 'Malayan Scouts' had been dropped and the unit renamed 22nd SAS Regiment. The Special Air Service, at last, were back in the regular army.

My world tour of British Military Hospitals resumed in February 1952 when a recurring bout of malaria led to a visit to BMH Hamburg. However, the illness that had laid me low in Malaya returned with a vengeance in June 1952 and led to a 42 day stay in BMH Hannover.

One day I got drunk and got myself into trouble. With all the inevitable consequences I had to leave the Army. I went to Australia to start a new life, but that, as they say, is another story.